THE MAKING
OF A
MISSIONARY

THE MAKING OF A MISSIONARY

By

J. HERBERT KANE

School of World Mission
Trinity Evangelical Divinity School
Deerfield, Illinois

Baker Book House
Grand Rapids, Michigan

Copyright 1975 by
Baker Book House Company
ISBN: 0-8010-5358-7

First printing, May 1975
Second printing, September 1977
Third printing, August 1980
Fourth printing, August 1982

The content of this book is based on chapters 1, 2, and 10 of the author's book *Understanding Christian Missions*, copyright 1974 by Baker Book House Company. The Scripture quotations in this publication are from the Revised Standard Version Bible, copyright 1946, 1952, and 1971 by the Division of Christian Education, National Council of the Churches of Christ in the U.S.A. and used by permission.

PHOTOLITHOPRINTED BY CUSHING - MALLOY, INC.
ANN ARBOR, MICHIGAN, UNITED STATES OF AMERICA

To
Nancy and Betty

Contents

Preface

The 1960s were a turbulent period in American history. College students were boycotting classes, smashing furniture, and burning their draft cards. Harvey Cox was writing about the "Secular City" and the God-is-dead theologians were having a field day. Seminarians, interested only in social and political action, were predicting the approaching demise of the institutional church. Interest in Christian missions was so low that one had to reach up to touch bottom.

All that is behind us now. The city has turned out to be anything but secular. Indeed, it is now filled with astrology, necromancy, witchcraft, Satan worship, Eastern Mysticism, Zen Buddhism, Transcendental Meditation, and a host of other religious phenomena. People who ten years ago didn't believe in the existence of demons were recently standing in long lines waiting to see *The Exorcist*. As for God, the rumors of His death were grossly exaggerated. He appears to be well and very much alive. Once again the pundits were wrong. A few prophets of doom are still with us, but the so-called prophetic voice sounds more and more like a pathetic echo.

Interest in both church and missions is definitely on the increase and the coming decade may turn out to be the greatest period for world missions in the present century. Dr. David M. Howard, Missions Director of Inter-Varsity Christian Fellowship, writing in December 1974, said: "This fall I received more requests for help from Christian schools than in any previous period I can remember." The Reverend Wesley Gustafson, Candidate Secretary of the Evangelical Free Church, reports that he is in touch with eighteen-hundred young people who have expressed an interest in missionary service. Other mission boards report more candidates than they have funds to support. Conservative seminaries are bursting at the seams, and interest in Christian missions is the highest in many decades. The Urbana Missionary Convention of 1973 attracted fourteen thousand persons, most of them students. More than five thousand of them signed the missionary pledge indicating their interest in missions and their willingness to serve on the mission field. We may well be on the verge of a major breakthrough in Christian missions.

More exciting still is the interest in world missions on the part of the churches in the Third World. The All-Asia Missions Consultation in Korea in August 1973, the first of its kind, went on record saying, "We are compelled by the Holy Spirit to declare that we shall work towards the placing of at least two hundred new Asian missionaries by the end of 1974." Four months later, the All-Asia Student Missionary Convention in the Philippines attracted eight hundred students from all parts of Asia. Already there are more than three thousand missionaries from the Third World serving in a cross-cultural context in their own or foreign countries.

Of one thing we may be sure. The missionary mandate has not been rescinded, nor will it ever be until the end of time. The Good News of the Gospel must be preached in *all the world* and then—and only then—will the end come (Mt 24:14). In the meantime the missionary enterprise continues to be a live option to every follower of Jesus Christ.

J. Herbert Kane
Deerfield, Illinois
January 1975

1

The Making of the Missionary

David Livingstone said, "God had only one Son and He made that Son a missionary." Every missionary follows in the steps of the Son of God, who visited this planet two thousand years ago on a mission of redemption. He came to seek and to save and to give His life a ransom for many. Upon the completion of His mission He returned to His Father in heaven; but before He left He said to His apostles, "As the Father has sent me, even so I send you" (Jn 20:21).

The worldwide mission of the Christian church is rooted in the Incarnation and is part of God's redemptive purpose for the world. God is a missionary God. The Bible is a missionary book. The gospel is a missionary message. The church is a missionary institution. And when the church ceases to be missionary minded, it has denied its faith and betrayed its trust.

Every Christian is a witness; but not every Christian is a missionary in the professional sense of the term. Many are called but few are chosen. Missionaries are made, not born; and as in every worthwhile vocation the making process is long and difficult. It can even be discouraging; but those who persevere to the end find it to be a rewarding occupation, second to none in valor, excitement, and achievement.

Never were the demands on the missionary greater than they are today. We need men of wisdom, vision, courage, patience, sincerity, and humility. These qualities and others must be acquired and developed before the missionary ever sets his foot on foreign soil.

1

Part of his training is to acquire an understanding of Christian missions in all major aspects of the undertaking at home and overseas. He should know both the strengths and the weaknesses, the successes and the failures. Only so will he be able to avoid the mistakes of the past.

Myths Regarding Missions

There is a great deal of confused thinking these days with regard to various aspects of Christian missions. Church members continue to support missions, mostly with their money, sometimes with their prayers; but they seldom read literature dealing with missionary strategy and policy. Most of them know little or nothing about the progress of the past or the nature and extent of the problems that remain. Much of their information comes through the annual missionary conference, and that is usually more inspirational than informational. Hence the myths persist. In this section we can deal only with the more obvious myths.

1. The myth of the vanishing missionary. Many people believe that the missionary era is over and that the missionary belongs to a species soon to become extinct. The reasoning goes something like this: When the modern missionary movement got under way 250 years ago, it coincided with the thrust of Western imperialism into Asia, Africa, and Oceania. During the heyday of imperialism Christian missions worked in cooperation with the colonial governments, implementing and supplementing their programs of educational and social reform. World War II marked the end of the colonial period; and except for a few pockets of colonialism here and there the system is forever dead. The gunboats have been recalled and the white sahibs have all gone home. The Christian missionaries should do the same. This reasoning is common.

Every time there is a riot or a revolution with anti-Western overtones, someone is sure to demand the withdrawal of the missionaries. Even without riot and revolution there are those who insist that the missionaries represent the last vestiges of Western imperialism, and as such should be recalled. To clinch the matter they ask: "If the national governments can function without the colonial administrators, why can't the national churches get along without the missionaries?" To all such people the missionaries at best are superfluous; at worst, they are downright dangerous. In either case, they should have the good sense to come home; or they should be recalled.

Our reply is twofold. First, the missionary's identification with imperialism was one of the unfortunate accidents of history. They did not plan it that way and were happy when the unholy alliance was terminated. If, as the critics say, it was a mistake for them to go in with the colonialists, surely it would have been a mistake to come out with them. Two wrongs don't make a right. To have come out with the colonialists would have confirmed what the nationalists and the Communists have been saying all along.

Second, the missionary task has not been completed. There is still an enormous amount of work to be done. To call it quits now would be to jeopardize all that has been accomplished up to this point. To compare the national government with the national church is grossly unfair to the latter. The former is in control of the entire country and has the support of all the people. Moreover, it has access to sufficient funds to implement its programs regardless of the cost. By contrast the national church in some countries represents only 1 or 2 percent of the population. To maintain its existing work strains the budget to the limit. In all such places the missionary will be needed and wanted for years to come. In many parts of the non-Christian world church membership is barely keeping up with the population growth; in other parts it is falling behind. There are twice as many non-Christians in India today as there were when William Carey arrived in 1793. By no stretch of the imagination is the missionary a vanishing species.

2. The myth of the foreign missionary. Jesus told us that the field is the world (Mt 13:38); but we have divided the field into two parts, home and foreign. In the popular mind a missionary is a person who is called by God to preach the gospel in a *foreign* country. The fellow who does the same kind of work at home must settle for a less exotic appellation.

> This mythology projected the illusion that the primary missionary frontier was geographical. And so developed what might be called the mystical doctrine of salt water. The mission of the church was so closely identified with geographical expansion, and the missionary enterprise so exclusively considered in terms of geographical frontiers, that the term "mission" inevitably had a foreign connotation. Traveling over salt water was thereby gradually changed from being the obvious concomitant of *some* kinds of missionary service, to being the *sine qua non* of *any* kind of missionary endeavor, and finally to being the final test and criterion of what in fact was missionary. Being transported over salt water, the more the better, was given a certain absolute theological and spiritual value.[1]

---

[1] Keith R. Bridston, *Mission Myth and Reality* (New York: Friendship Press, 1965), pp. 32-33.

There is, of course, a great difference between preaching the gospel to Americans in Chicago, Los Angeles, or New York and preaching to the Auca Indians of Ecuador. The latter requires insights, attitudes, and skills not necessary for the successful prosecution of the former. In that sense and to that degree there is something "special" about the missionary who serves in a cross-cultural situation. It does not, however, justify the degree to which we have exalted the foreign missionary and played down the home missionary. Both are missionaries in the true sense of the word and deserve similar treatment.

The preference we show for foreign missions can be seen in our treatment of missionary candidates. Most candidates are required to raise their own support before proceeding to the field. Candidates looking forward to foreign service generally raise their support without much difficulty. Home mission candidates usually take much longer.

Somehow the home churches have surrounded foreign missions with an aura of sacredness not granted to any other form of Christian service. This is unfortunate, for it not only violates the principles of the New Testament, but it also polarizes the missionary enterprise into two separate entities, one superior to the other.

American churches give tens of thousands of dollars every year to mission projects in every continent except North America. Church members will travel thousands of miles to Quito, Ecuador, to see Radio Station HCJB that they have been helping to support, but they feel no obligation to support WMBI in Chicago. The only difference is that one represents foreign missions and the other home missions, and foreign missions usually win out.

It is becoming increasingly difficult to maintain the arbitrary difference between home and foreign missions. We used to think that foreign missions was more difficult and dangerous than home missions, and that a person took his life in his hand if he went to the jungles of Borneo, Amazon, or New Guinea. Today there are few places on the mission field as difficult or dangerous as the ghettos of our large American cities. Any pastor who leaves a wealthy suburban church for Christian service in the inner city is by any definition a missionary. Such an assignment is likely to require more courage, more faith, and more perseverance than most posts on the foreign field.

3. The myth of the ugly missionary. The term *missionary* was once a cherished word. Today it has lost its glamor. Indeed, there are those who suggest that the term should be dropped. It smacks too much, they say, of colonialism. Strange as it may seem, the friends at home are the only ones that have this hang-up. Apparently the term is not a dirty word in the Third World. The church leaders there certainly have no objection to it.

In 1964 Daniel T. Niles, outstanding leader of the Younger Churches of Asia, made a strong plea for "old-time missionaries" not only to remain in Asia but to take the initiative in church affairs. He said:

> We are not looking for fraternal helpers. We want missionaries. We know that you cannot find too many of them, but at least send us some. I am not against fraternal helpers. I am only protesting that they are not missionaries. They are helpers. We need any amount of help; but it is the missionary that is wanted, and wanted badly.[2]

The same is true of the political leaders. When the African colonies got their independence in the 1960s leader after leader went on public record thanking the missionaries for their contribution to independence and asking them to remain at their posts to help build the new nation. Of all the expatriates living in the Third World, the missionaries and the Peace Corps are the only ones there to give and not to get; and the national leaders know this.

The missionary, though held in high esteem by his friends and converts on the mission field, has never stood very high in the social register in his own hometown. The mental image conjured up by the word *missionary* was anything but flattering. The usual cartoon depicted him as wearing knee sox, Bermuda shorts, and a beat-up pith helmet. The word *missionary* needn't appear; the identity was complete. The missionary wife looked even worse. She was expected to have flat heels, long skirt, white blouse, and a bun at the back of her neck. The children, with their hand-me-downs, scuffed shoes, and unruly behavior, completed the picture.

Intellectually the picture wasn't much brighter. Not many missionaries had college degrees. For this reason the critics assumed that they were doomed to mediocrity. Some even went so far as to suggest that they volunteered for overseas service because they couldn't make the grade at home. Brainy men and pretty women were not supposed to be missionaries!

The fact of the matter is that missionaries are neither dumb nor dowdy. Immediately upon return to the States the entire family in many cases is given a clothing allowance which enables them to get a whole new wardrobe. Today it is virtually impossible to spot a visiting missionary in a Sunday morning service unless he is on the platform. The womenfolk are smartly dressed and compare favorably with their homeside sisters. As for the MKs, their problem is to figure out a way to look as unkempt as their city cousins!

When it comes to intellectual prowess the missionary is not one whit behind the average American. A missionary without a college

---

[2] Dougles Webster, *Yes to Mission* (New York: Seabury Press, 1966), p. 31.

degree is a rare person today. Many have two or three degrees. He may not remember whether the New York Mets are in the American League or the National League; but he knows more about geography, history, and world affairs than we do. While away from our affluent society he acquired a genuine appreciation for the simpler, finer things of life. He can converse intelligently on a wide range of subjects and is an expert on his adopted country—its history, people, and culture.

As for the MKs, they may be less sophisticated than our youngsters, but they are more mature. They have read more books, visited more places, talked to more people, and made more friends. They are usually bicultural and can speak at least two languages fluently. They are accustomed to world travel, which in itself is an education. They have experienced in real life the exciting and exotic things available to us only on television. The number of MKs who go on to college, and do well when they get there, is considerably higher than for the population as a whole. Most of them go into the professions—law, medicine, politics, the pastorate, and teaching. Not a few return to the field as missionaries. Very few have any desire to go into business simply to make money and live well.

4. The myth of the spiritual missionary. We have placed the missionary on a pedestal. We have admired his zeal, his courage, his dedication, and his humility. We have praised him for his spirit of sacrifice, his sense of duty, his willingness to take joyfully the spoiling of his goods and the destruction of his property. And the ultimate in self-sacrifice was his willingness to part with his children at the tender age of six in order to pursue a missionary career. To cap it all he lived by faith, looking to the Lord alone for the supply of his daily needs; and he did all this quietly and joyfully with no thought of reward.

We took for granted that anyone who could do all these things must be a spiritual giant. He must live always in fellowship with God. Prayer must indeed be his vital breath, his native air. Surely he must have achieved such a high degree of personal holiness as to be beyond the temptations that assail the common Christian. He must long since have gained the victory over the world, the flesh, and the devil. Such a person, we concluded, must be a saint.

Well, we were wrong, and the missionary would be the first to acknowledge the fact. There were, and are, spiritual giants among them, but the *average* missionary is a man of like passions with ourselves (Ja 5:17). He is fashioned from the same clay and he, like us, has the treasure of the gospel in an earthen vessel (2 Co 4:7). He may have a heart of gold, but he has feet of clay. When he lets his hair down he looks very much like the rest of us. He is basically a spiritual man, but he has his full share of idiosyncrasies. He has his headaches and his hang-ups, his blind spots and his pet peeves, his prejudices and his passions. He even has his doubts and fears. Touch him and he's touchy. Cross him and he gets cross. There are limits to his endurance. He has cracked up physically, mentally, morally, and spiritually and has had to come home to an unsympathetic constituency devoid of understanding. He has been known to fall into sin, including adultery, homosexuality, and suicide. Not all missionaries are happily married; they have domestic problems. Not all MKs turn out well. Some of them go astray. Some resent the fact that their parents are missionaries. Some become rebellious and join the hippies. A few have been known to end up as agnostics or alcoholics.

The missionary, like the apostle Paul, lives by the grace of God (1 Co 15:10) and cherishes the hope that by a process of divine alchemy the infirmities of his flesh will become an occasion for the manifestation of the power of Christ (2 Co 12:9). In and of himself he can do nothing (Jn 15:5). With and through Christ he can do all things (Ph 4:13). Others may have illusions about the missionary; he has none about himself. He understands all too well the truth of those lines by Henry Twells:

> O Savior Christ, our woes dispel;
>   For some are sick, and some are sad,
> And some have never loved Thee well,
>   And some have lost the love they had.
>
> And none, O Lord, have perfect rest,
>   For none are wholly free from sin;
> And they who fain would serve Thee best
>   Are conscious most of wrong within.

5. The myth of the specialized missionary. We hear much these days about specialization in all fields of human endeavor. Automation and cybernation make it possible for more and more tasks to be performed by fewer and fewer highly skilled people in key positions. Before long only the specialists will be able to find employment. By the year 2000 only 10 percent of the work force will be employed. The other 90 percent will be paid by the government to do nothing!

There is no doubt about it—specialization is the name of the game. Wherein then lies the myth? There are really two myths, not one, so far as missionary work is concerned.

The first myth is the idea that the day of the general missionary is over; now only specialists need apply. Indeed, there seems to be a conspiracy to downgrade the general missionary in favor of the specialist. The general missionary is regarded as a jack-of-all-trades and therefore master of none. As such he is definitely a second-class worker in the vineyard of the Lord.

There is some misunderstanding at this point. The truth of the matter is that from the beginning of the missionary movement we have had both general and specialized missionaries. There is no rivalry between them. The one supplements and complements the other.

What people don't understand is that the East is still several decades behind the West and the need for specialists there is not so great as it is here. Moreover, there are not enough missionaries to permit the missions to indulge in the luxury of specialization.

A good seminary in the United States will probably have two or three professors in the New Testament department, and the Old Testament department will have the same. These men teach only in the area of their concentration. But on the mission field, where the average seminary has twenty-five students and only two or three full-time faculty members, it is obvious that specialization, however desirable, is out of the question. The Old Testament professor will be asked to teach homiletics and apologetics in addition to Old Testament. The church history man will be required to teach evangelism and missions as well as church history.

For this reason mission executives prefer men who are versatile and flexible. Indeed, versatility is the greatest single human virtue any missionary can possess. Without it he may feel like a square peg in a round hole and blame the mission for his feelings of frustration.

The same goes for the medical missionary. The doctor on the mission field must be both a physician and a surgeon, for often he is the only doctor on the hospital staff. The heart, eye, and bone specialists will have ample scope for their special skills, but they must be prepared to function as general practitioners. Indeed, most mission doctors have to pitch in and help solve the problem when there is a short in the electrical system or when the incubator, the jeep, or the X-ray machine breaks down. At such times versatility is a priceless asset. Some doctors have been known to build their own hospitals!

The other myth is the idea that only doctors, nurses, teachers, radio technicians, agriculturalists, etc., are specialists. All others are lumped together and referred to as general missionaries. Is the evangelist not a specialist? What about the seminary professor, the youth worker, the business manager, or the area superintendent? Are they not specialists? If a man has four years of medical school we call him a specialist. If another man spends three or four years in a seminary, he is a general missionary. This doesn't make sense.

6. The myth of the primitive life. There are people who believe that missionaries live in primitive conditions with barely enough to keep body and soul together. They still think of them as hacking their way through snake-infested jungles and living in thatched houses with furniture made from packing cases.

There are, of course, some missionaries who live that way. Wycliffe Bible Translators and the New Tribes Mission, because of the nature of their work, have most of their missionaries living and working in primitive conditions. In fact, part of their training takes place in a jungle camp where they are required to survive for several weeks in the jungle equipped only with a sleeping bag, a machete, a compass, a few simple medicines, and a box of matches.

But they are the exception. The great majority of present-day missionaries enjoys a standard of living considerably higher than they ever anticipated. They are located in modern cities where they drive their own cars, shop in department stores and supermarkets, and have access to four-lane highways, airports, public libraries, golf courses, and tennis courts. Even the missionaries living in bush country usually congregate in central stations built for the purpose, where they have the basic amenities of Western civilization—simple but adequate housing, running water, and indoor plumbing. Most of them have electricity even if they have to generate it themselves. This enables them to make use of various kinds of electrical appliances brought from home. Food, mail, medicine, gasoline, and other supplies are flown in periodically by Mission Aviation Fellowship planes.

A young missionary couple that went to Ethiopia only last summer wrote in their first prayer letter:

> The S.I.M. station is beautiful. Gardens abound with all the familiar fruits and vegetables plus such things as bananas, pineapples, and papayas. Flowers are abundant. One can view Jimma five km. away with several mountain ranges in the background. The homes have electricity, running water, flush toilets, and refrigerators. Carey and Livingstone should have seen this day![3]

In former days the missions acquired land and built homes for their missionaries which were rent free. These were invariably Western in architectural style and interior decoration. They were large, airy, and comfortable. In fact some of these homes were better than some parsonages here in the United States.

In more recent years it has become a practice for missionaries to live in rented premises. These are usually located in the more attractive part of town and would compare favorably with middle-class housing in urban America.

---

[3] Letter from Art and Sue Volkmann, September 1973.

God forbid that we should base our missionary appeal to modern youth on creature comforts; but truthfulness demands that we tell it like it is. When most missionaries first leave for the field they are prepared to live and work under any circumstances; but when they get there they are pleasantly surprised to find conditions much better than they had ever dreamed.

7. The myth of the hungry heart. Few Christians have an adequate understanding of the enormous difficulties inherent in the conversion of the non-Christian peoples of the world. It is assumed that the "heathen" in their moral and spiritual degradation are expectantly awaiting the coming of the missionary; his arrival will be the signal for them to abandon their evil ways and embrace the gospel.

Missionary speakers, literature, and hymns have all contributed to this view. The "heathen" have been depicted as sitting in darkness, living in fear, and dying without hope. They have been variously described as forsaken, benighted, depraved, debauched, and deluded. Much has been made of the phenomenon of fear—fear of sickness, ancestors, evil spirits, angry gods, natural disasters, and finally, death.

Surely these people in their more sober moments must be aware of their plight. Given an opportunity they will readily accept the Christian message with its offer of life, health, joy, peace, and power.

What are the facts? That the non-Christian peoples of the world are lost in the darkness of sin, living in fear, and dying without hope is true. That they are ready and eager to accept Christ is not true. From time to time missionaries have come across certain individuals who believed the gospel the first time they heard it. They are the exception, not the rule. The overwhelming majority of non-Christian peoples must be included in Paul's statement: "None is righteous, no, not one; no one understands, no one seeks for God. All have turned aside, together they have gone wrong; no one does good, not even one" (Ro 3:10-12).

There is no evidence to support the view expressed in a well-known missionary hymn to the effect that "the heathen in his blindness" is calling on us to "deliver him from error's chain." He is not aware of his blindness, nor does he feel the weight of any chain. The Hindu, the Buddhist, the Muslim, and the Confucianist all consider their religion superior to ours; hence they are in no hurry to give it up. As for the peasant in his paddy field, he is so engrossed in the problem of feeding his large family that he has neither time nor thought for the needs of his soul. His chief concern is not where he will spend eternity, but how he and his children will survive until harvest. The same goes for the shopkeeper in the bazaar, the worker in the factory, and the housewife in the home. And if the time comes when they do need the comforts of religion, they will turn to their own priests and gods, not to the foreign missionary.

If anyone is inclined to doubt these remarks, he need only recall the fact that after a hundred years of missionary work in Japan, there are only one million professing Christians out of a population of 107 million. The figures for other countries in Asia are not much better; in some instances they are worse. We take to these people the bread of life only to find they're not hungry. We offer them the water of life only to discover they're not thirsty.

8. The myth of the closing door. In this postcolonial period a great deal has been said about closing doors. Books and magazine articles have discussed the problem from every conceivable angle. Missionaries on furlough have added to the confusion by warning us that we have "five more years" in one part of the world and "ten more years" in another. We seem to have developed a pathological preoccupation with this particular problem. In fact we have talked so long and loudly about closing doors that we have come to believe our own story.

It would be foolish, of course, to deny that some doors have already closed or that others will close in the future. What we do deny is that sooner or later *all* doors will close ¡and the missionaries will find themselves without employment. Neither the lessons of history nor the statements of Scripture oblige us to accept that melancholy conclusion.

If one takes the trouble to enumerate all the countries that during the past twenty-five years have closed their doors to Christian missionaries, he will find that his list is rather short. In Asia it will include China, North Korea, North Vietnam, and Burma. In the Middle East it will include Libya, Syria, Iraq, and Southern Yemen. To his surprise he will find not a single closed country in Black Africa, Latin America, or Oceania. So his list will include only eight or ten countries, and there are 141 countries in the United Nations.

Some Muslim countries, such as Malaysia, Morocco, Algeria, and Sudan, are not happy with the missionaries now in those countries and may expel them in the days to come. On the other hand some countries, such as Nepal, Somalia, and Yemen, have in recent years accepted missionaries for the first time. Somalia has had second thoughts and more recently has terminated mission work. Afghanistan is closed to professional missionaries but had allowed over one hundred nonprofessional missionaries to engage in medical and educational work before the Russian incursion.

Some countries, such as Indonesia, Kenya, and India, that we feared would close, are still open. Others, such as Ethiopia and Colombia, that were closed for several years, are open again. It is quite possible that other countries may do the same. We dare not write off even Red China.

And what shall be said about the 100-plus countries that are open? In some of them the work is difficult and the response is disappointing, but in many of them the missionaries describe the opportunities as "fabulous" and "fantastic." The United Bible Societies are publishing and distributing the Scriptures in over 150 countries. The Assemblies of God Mission has work in 92 countries. The Moody Literature Mission is producing and distributing gospel literature in 184 languages in over 100 countries. In addition the Moody Institute of Science has made its films available in 21 languages to missionaries in 120 countries of the world. If worldwide missionary activity is any criterion, it doesn't look as if the doors are closing.

9. The myth of the finished task. Missionary speakers have much to say these days about the indigenous churches on the mission field which are reported to be self-governing, self-propagating, and self-supporting. And the question is raised: If the national churches are able to stand on their own feet, pay their own way, and manage their own affairs, why are missionaries still needed? This is a good question.

We should blush with shame should we have to confess that after 250 years of missionary work we had not yet produced any indigenous churches. The indigenous churches are indeed a fact. Some are large and strong; others are small and weak. We thank God for every one of them. When we remember the enormous difficulties of the pioneer days, we are amazed that so much was accomplished by so few. Every indigenous church is a monument to the grace of God and the power of the gospel.

But having said that, we must go on to state that the missionary mandate has not been fulfilled when we have established indigenous churches. The original mandate called for the evangelization of the world, which includes preaching the gospel to *every* creature and making disciples of *all* nations. And this performance must be repeated in every succeeding generation. *That* task is far from complete.

In some countries, such as Korea and Indonesia, the national churches are large and strong; but even there the Christians represent not more than 10 percent of the population. These churches are certainly able to maintain their own existence, but can they be expected to win the other 90 percent of the population without outside help?

And what about the other countries where the churches are small and weak and the Christians account for only 2 or 3 percent of the population? The churches in Japan are strong from some points of view, but weak from others; the Christians there represent less than 1 percent of the total population. The Japanese church lacks evangelistic vision and zeal. Even the evangelical churches insist that the missionaries make the best evangelists.

In Thailand the situation is even less hopeful. For every Christian there are 999 Buddhists, most of whom are still without a knowledge of Jesus Christ. The Baptist church in Burma is very strong, but it is composed entirely of tribespeople, converts from animism. The 28 million Burmese who are Buddhists are practically untouched after 160 years of Christian work. Not more than 10,000 of them are Christians.

The Scriptures have been translated into 1,526 languages and dialects, but the complete Bible is available in only 255 languages. This means that millions of church members in the Third World have only the New Testament, and many of them don't even have that. Wycliffe Bible Translators estimates that there are 2,000 tribes, representing 160 million people, who are still without any portion of the Word of God. Indeed, their languages have not yet been reduced to writing.

According to the most reliable estimates world Christianity is not holding its own against the non-Christian religions. In 1960 the Christians represented about 34 percent of the world's population. Today the figure is around 30 percent and it continues to drop slowly year by year. There are more non-Christians in the two countries of China and India than there are Christians in the entire world.

Obviously the task of world evangelization is not complete. The indigenous churches still need help. In spite of all we have accomplished in the last 250 years we have barely scratched the surface.

What Is a Missionary?

The word *missionary* comes from the Latin word *mitto*, which means "to send." It is the equivalent of the Greek word *apostello*, which also means "to send." The root meaning of the two words is identical.

The word *apostle* occurs more than eighty times in the New Testament. In one place it refers to Christ (He 3:1). Jesus Christ was the first Apostle. He was also the chief Apostle. He derived His apostleship from the Father who, He said on many occasions, "sent" Him into the world on a mission of redemption.

From among His disciples Jesus chose twelve men whom He called "apostles." These men were taught and trained by Him, endowed with apostolic authority, and after the Resurrection were sent out to make disciples of all nations (Mt 28:18-20). There was a direct connection between His mission and theirs (Jn 20:21). These men came to be known as "The Twelve." They were undoubtedly a unique group of men with unique privileges and responsibilities. But there were others in the New Testament who came to be referred to as "apostles." Included in this second group were such well-known men as Barnabas, Timothy, Silas, and others.

In The Acts the apostles are sent out by the Holy Spirit (Acts 13:4) *and* the church (Acts 13:3). Most of Luke's account is built around the activities of the apostles, though they were by no means the only ones who preached the gospel (Acts 8:4; 11:19).

To whom should the term *missionary* be applied? Obviously today's missionary is not in the same class with the twelve apostles, who must forever remain in a class by themselves (Lk 22:30; Re 21:14). They do, however, have much in common with the "second-string" apostles who were sent out by the various churches on teaching and preaching missions to all parts of the Roman Empire. They did not remain long in any one place, but moved about as the Spirit directed them (Acts 8:26, 29, 39; 16:6-7).

It is impossible to come up with a scientific definition of the term *missionary* that will meet all the conditions and satisfy all the demands. It is possible to punch holes in any definition on which we might settle. In the traditional sense the term *missionary* has been reserved for those who have been called by God to a full-time ministry of the Word and prayer (Acts 6:4), and who have crossed geographical and/or cultural boundaries (Acts 22:21) to preach the gospel in those areas of the world where Jesus Christ is largely, if not entirely, unknown (Ro 15:20). This definition, though by no means perfect, has the virtue of being Biblical.

The problem is more than a semantic one and must be seen in a much larger frame of reference. There are those who refuse to buy the idea of "full-time Christian service" as applied to pastors, evangelists, and missionaries. By their definition every dedicated Christian, regardless of his vocation, is in full-time Christian service. If every Christian is in full-time service, then it is only a step to saying, as many do today, that every Christian is a missionary.

There is abroad in evangelical circles a move to do away with all "artificial distinctions." Today's Christians are challenged to rethink their position and give up their narrow view of the Christian life with its rigid categories of black and white and right and wrong, and to embrace a more sophisticated view of the wholeness of life. Gone are the former dichotomies between the secular and the sacred, work and prayer, and service and witness. As for any special missionary call—forget it. All Christians are missionaries.

The above point of view is not entirely wrong. It contains an element of truth that needs to be acknowledged and emphasized. On the other hand, if pushed too far it can become dangerous. Take the matter of tithing. There are those who assert that tithing is too legalistic an approach to Christian stewardship. They claim that "everything belongs to God" and they would not think of giving Him only a tenth of their income. Such talk sounds very spiritual and certainly it is not contrary to the Word of God; but what really matters is the end result. When December 31 comes around, how much of one's income has actually been spent on oneself and how much has been given to the work of the Lord? It is difficult to understand how $2,000 spent on a winter vacation in Acapulco or $50,000 spent on a beautiful yacht can be regarded as going into the Lord's work. James, the leader of the Jerusalem church, had some harsh words for Christians who spend their money on luxury and pleasure (Ja 5:1-5). There is no suggestion that God regards such money as going into His work. It is better to settle for a "legalistic" system of tithing and see to it that God actually gets His tenth, than to make all kinds of pious protests about everything belonging to the Lord and ending up by giving Him less than He demands.

The same principle applies to the use of the term *missionary*. There are those who advocate that we drop the word altogether. Others insist that it should be applied to all committed Christians. Stephen Neill has warned that if everybody is a missionary, nobody is a missionary. The Chinese have a proverb: "If two men feed a horse, it will lose weight; if two men keep a boat, it will soon leak." What is everybody's job is nobody's job. If every Christian is a missionary, missionary work is bound to suffer. It is correct to say that every Christian is, or should be, a witness. It is not correct to say that every Christian is a missionary.

An illustration may help at this point. During World War II there was in this country total mobilization. No sector of the economy, private or public, was exempt from the war effort. Whether a person was driving a truck, or digging ditches, or filing vouchers, he was part of the total war effort. But none of these persons was in the same category as the men in uniform, who were known as "soldiers." This term was not applied to everyone, not even to the workers in the munitions factories. It was reserved for the twelve million men under arms in the various branches of the Armed Services. Many of them never saw combat; some never even went overseas. The fact remains that by government statute they were in a class by themselves and played a unique role in the conduct of the war. No one suggested that "everybody" was a soldier. Soldiers were soldiers and civilians were civilians, even though both were totally involved in the war effort and, win or lose, shared the same fate.

The same kind of distinction should be made in the spiritual warfare in which we are engaged. The total resources of the Christian church should be thrown into the battle for the souls of men on a global scale, and every member of that church should regard himself as being involved in the total mobilization required by such an operation. But not every church member is a missionary. That term should be reserved for those who, like the soldiers in Uncle Sam's army, necessarily fill a unique role in the overall operation. In this sense it is helpful to retain the term *missionary* and to invest it with full and proper significance.

When we say that the missionary fills a unique role we do not imply that he is better than others, simply that he is different. He is not necessarily more spiritual than the pastor, or even the layman, who remains at home. Nor will his reward at the judgment seat of Christ be any greater. He is the servant of Christ and will be asked the same questions and judged on the same basis as anyone else. Did he seek to promote his own glory or was he concerned solely for the glory of God (1 Co 10:31)? Was he motivated by some personal considerations or was he constrained by the love of Christ (1 Co 13:1-3)? Did he do his work in the energy of the flesh or in the power of the Holy Spirit (Acts 1:8)? If he can answer all three questions correctly he will have his reward; otherwise his work will be judged to be wood, hay, and stubble to be consumed in the fire (1 Co 3:12-15). The missionary is not better than his fellow workers, just different.

The missionary in a cross-cultural situation finds himself filling several important roles.

1. He is an ambassador for Christ. The American missionary carries a little green book called a passport. It is issued by the State Department in Washington. It is his most precious possession. Without it he couldn't enter the country of his choice or get back into the United States. The American missionary is proud to be an American and is grateful for the services his government is prepared to offer, especially in time of war or revolution. That he is an American citizen is quite incidental to his mission. He might just as well be a Canadian or a Norwegian. More important is the fact that he is an ambassador for Christ.

His Sovereign is the Son of God who, in the Incarnation, became the Son of Man, that through His death and resurrection He might become the Savior and Sovereign of the world. One purpose of the incarnation was to bind the Strong Man, Satan (Mt 12:25-29), to destroy his works (1 Jn 3:8), his power (He 2:14), and ultimately his person (Re 20:10). By virtue of His glorious ascension He is now sitting on the right hand of the Majesty on high, far above all principality, and power, and might, and dominion (Eph 1:21). All power in heaven and on earth has been given to Him (Mt 28:18). By raising Him from the dead and exalting Him at His own right hand, God has forever established the universal Lordship of Jesus Christ (Acts 2:36). He is not only the Head of the church; He is also the Lord of history, the King of the nations, and the Judge of all the earth. In short, Jesus Christ is King of kings and Lord of lords. Sooner or later all men and nations must come to terms with Him (Ph 2:9-11).

To this end the King has given orders to His ambassadors. They are to go into all the world, preach the gospel to every creature, and make disciples of all nations (Mt 28:19). All men everywhere are required to repent and believe the gospel (Acts 17:30). Only by so doing can they be delivered from the dominion of darkness and be transferred to the kingdom of light (Co 1:13). Nothing short of world conquest is the ultimate goal, and the King has given assurance that one day the kingdoms of this world are to become the Kingdom of our Lord and of His Christ (Re 11:15). There is no ambiguity about the plan, no uncertainty about the outcome.

> Jesus shall reign where'er the sun
> Doth its successive journeys run;
> His Kingdom spread from shore to shore
> Till moons shall wax and wane no more.

The lowly missionary is the personal envoy of the Sovereign of the universe. His abode, even should it be a mud hut in Africa, a snow-covered house in Alaska, a cottage in the Amazon jungle, or a tent in the Gobi Desert, is the "residency over which waves the banner of his King and round which an angel keeps watch."

> This must ever be holy ground, even though all round be evil, for the Embassy is privileged land and here the Ambassador enjoys extra-territorial rights. No one may interfere in the correspondence and intercourse between him and his King. . . . His intercourse with his Sovereign is so safeguarded that no spy can overhear his reports or intercept his dispatches. At any moment of the day or night he may have audience with his King, secure His counsel, receive His instructions, and can never fail of His understanding sympathy.[4]

While the missionary has none of the outward accoutrements

[4] Mildred Cable and Francesca French, *Ambassadors for Christ* (London: Hodder and Stoughton, 1935), p. 153.

usually associated with diplomatic protocol, nevertheless his credentials are impeccable. He is the bearer of a divine revelation enshrined in an infallible Book. He has the law of God in his mouth, the rod of God in his hand, and the power of God in his life. His message, given to him by his Sovereign, he delivers without fear, favor, or flattery. The message itself is both clear and simple. In former times God allowed all nations to walk in their own ways (Acts 14:16); but since He has acted decisively in Jesus Christ He now commands all men everywhere to repent (Acts 17:30), to turn from their dumb idols to the true and living God (1 Th 1:9), and to acknowledge the universal Lordship of Jesus Christ (Ph 2:9-11).

2. **He is a herald of truth.** Jesus Christ claimed to be the way, the truth, and the life (Jn 14:6). He promised that men would know the truth and the truth would make them free (Jn 8:32). He stated that His purpose in coming into the world was to bear witness to the truth (Jn 18:37). His kingdom is a kingdom of truth (Jn 18:36-37). It is founded on an understanding of the truth (Jn 8:32). It is extended by the preaching of the truth (Co 1:5-6). It is maintained by the practice of the truth (1 Jn 4:1-6).

The missionary as an ambassador for Christ becomes a herald of truth. When Jesus sent out the twelve apostles on their first preaching mission He gave them clear instructions: "What I tell you in the dark, utter in the light and what you hear whispered, proclaim upon the housetops" (Mt 10:27). The idea of a herald is that of a town crier before the days of mass communications. He marched the length and breadth of the town reading aloud a proclamation for the benefit of the townsfolk. He did not invent or originate the message. He simply proclaimed it. This is the responsibility of the missionary. He does not invent his message any more than Paul did (Ga 1:1-10). He has been told precisely what he is to teach and preach: all that Jesus commanded (Mt 28:20). That includes all His major discourses, public and private, including the Sermon on the Mount.

The modern missionary finds himself in an embarrassing situation. In a pluralistic world it is becoming increasingly difficult to maintain the truth of the gospel as over against the other faiths. It is considered bad taste to suggest that one religion is true and all the other religions are partly or wholly false. No religion, we are told, has all the truth and nothing but the truth; and to cling to such an outmoded concept is to forfeit one's intellectual respectability. What is needed, they say, is an eclectic religion that will incorporate the best elements of the various faiths, including Christianity.

At the risk of being misunderstood the Christian missionary, in all humility and sincerity, must insist on the truth of the gospel. If other religions contradict Christianity they must be regarded as false, at least at the point of contradiction. Two contradictory statements on any subject cannot both be true. Both *may* be wrong. One *must* be wrong. The Christian faith is not true because the missionary says so, but because Jesus Christ, the King of truth, declared it to be so.

This question of truth is of immense importance. Stephen Neill said: "The only reason for being a Christian is the overpowering conviction that the Christian faith is true."[5]

That expression "overwhelming conviction" describes perfectly the mentality of the early church. The apostles believed with all their hearts that in the gospel of Christ they possessed the truth concerning God, man, sin, and salvation. By that truth they were determined to live; for that truth they were prepared to die. Jesus Christ was the way, the truth, and the life; and there was salvation only in Him. So far as the apostles were concerned there were many paths, but only one way; many prophets, but only one Savior; many religions, but only one gospel.

Their creed was simple but it was sufficient: "Jesus Christ is Lord." He stands in a class all by Himself. He occupies a solitary throne. He has no equals; He doesn't even have any rivals. And they came to this conclusion slowly, cautiously, painfully over a period of three years, during which time they saw Him under every conceivable condition of life. And the Resurrection clinched the matter for them. It was no "Easter story" that they believed, but a historic event of which they were eyewitnesses. They were there when it happened; it happened to them; and they were never the same again. The Resurrection is the keystone in the arch of the Christian faith. If it is a fact, Christianity is true; if it is not a fact, Christianity is false. The resurrection of Christ is one of the best authenticated facts of history. There is more and better evidence for the resurrection of Jesus than for the death of Socrates.

As a herald of truth it is the missionary's solemn but joyous task to proclaim to the entire non-Christian world the glorious news that Jesus Christ lived and died and rose again, and by so doing provided salvation for the whole human race. As a result whosoever will now call on the name of the Lord will be saved.

3. He is an apostle of love. Christianity is preeminently a religion of love. God loved the world and gave His Son (Jn 3:16). Jesus loved the world and gave Himself (Ga 2:20). Christians are called upon to do the same (1 Jn 3:16). Jesus said, "By this all men will know that you are my disciples, if you have love for one another" (Jn 13:35).

---

[5] Stephen Neill, *Call to Mission* (Philadelphia: Fortress Press, 1970), p. 10.

According to the apostle Paul love is the supreme virtue. It gives value to all the other virtues of the Christian life (1 Co 13:1-3). Indeed, without love the other virtues count for nothing.

As Christ was the embodiment of God's love, so the missionary is the embodiment of Christ's love. Jesus wept over the city of Jerusalem when it failed to respond to God's love. Paul could say of his unresponsive compatriots: "I have great sorrow and unceasing anguish in my heart. For I could wish that I myself were accursed and cut off from Christ for the sake of my brethren, my kinsmen by race" (Ro 9:2-3). And these very "kinsmen" were the ones who, time and again, tried to destroy him.

Missionaries have always been apostles of love. Count Zinzendorf, the greatest missionary statesman of the eighteenth century, said: "I have one passion, it is He and He alone." Hudson Taylor, who gave fifty years to the service of Christ in China, said: "If I had a thousand lives, I'd give them all to China." Alexander Mackay, writing to the Church Missionary Society, said: "My heart burns for the deliverance of Africa." Melville Cox died after being in Liberia only four months. His last words were: "Let a thousand fall before Africa be given up." Henry Martyn on his arrival in India said, "Now let me burn out for God." All these men were, like Paul, constrained by the love of Christ (2 Co 5:14) and they literally burned themselves out for God and man.

Nor was this love confined to a passion for *souls*. With the love of God poured into their hearts by the Holy Spirit (Ro 5:5), they overflowed with love to others—not just their souls, but their bodies as well. They loved them as persons, not just as potential converts; and they tried to minister to the needs of the whole man: body, mind, and soul.

The missionaries went where others would not go, and remained with the people they loved through famine, flood, plague, pestilence, and war. Often they endangered their own lives to save the lives of others. They may not have raised the dead; but they healed the sick, fed the poor, and clothed the naked. They cared for widows and orphans. They took in abandoned baby girls, fed, clothed, and educated them, and, when the time came, arranged suitable marriages for them.

Hundreds of missionaries became martyrs. In the Boxer Rebellion in China the Overseas Missionary Fellowship lost seventy-nine missionaries and their children in one year. When the storm blew over the remaining missionaries returned to their stations, asking for nothing but the privilege of serving the people who had killed their colleagues. When compensation was offered by the Chinese government it was refused.

During the Sino-Japanese War (1937-1945) hundreds of missionaries, many of them single ladies, opened their homes and compounds to Chinese women and girls in an effort to save them from the rapacious Japanese soldiers. Hector MacMillan, father of five children, was killed by the Simbas in Zaire in 1964. Undaunted, his wife returned to Zaire in 1966 to minister to the very people who had killed her husband. Rachel Saint and Betty Elliot took the gospel to the Auca Indians who murdered the brother of one and the husband of the other. Today the Aucas are Christians. Two of the children of the martyred missionaries were baptized by the men who murdered their fathers. Such is the power of Christian love.

During his exile on the Island of St. Helena, Napoleon remarked to a friend: "Alexander, Charlemagne, and myself all tried to found an empire on force and we failed. Jesus Christ is building an empire on love, and today there are millions of people who would gladly die for His sake." The missionary, more than anyone else, is helping to build that kingdom of love.

4. He is an envoy of peace. One of Christ's Messianic titles is Prince of Peace (Is 9:6). At His birth the angels sang about "peace on earth" (Lk 2:14). In His teachings He advocated peace (Mt 5:21-26). By His death He achieved peace between God and man (Co 1:20) and between man and man (Eph 2:14-15). Every kingdom known to man was founded on force and maintained by force. His kingdom was different. He would not resort to force nor permit His disciples to do so (Jn 18:36). He extolled the virtues of peace and pronounced a benediction on those who actively seek peace (Mt 5:9).

The kingdom that Jesus Christ is building on earth is a kingdom of peace (Ro 14:17), and the gospel that goes along with that kingdom is a gospel of peace (Eph 6:15). This peace has two dimensions, vertical and horizontal. Traditionally the conservatives have emphasized the first, the liberals the second. Both are part of the gospel; both belong to the kingdom.

The missionary, by virtue of his high calling, must be an envoy of peace. He bids men be reconciled first to God (2 Co 5:20) and then to one another (Ro 12:18). Sin brought discord into the world and set man against God (Eph 4:17-19). It also set man against man (Ro 3:15-18). The Fall not only separated Adam and Eve from God but produced enmity between Cain and Abel. Before man can be reconciled to man, he must first be reconciled to God.

The missionary, when he preaches the gospel of peace, hopes to achieve both dimensions of peace—the horizontal and the vertical. Consequently wherever he has gone he has tried to sow the seeds of peace between warring factions. He more than anyone else has been able to bridge the gap between the Jew and the Gentile, the Arab and the Jew, the Hindu and the Muslim.

Before the coming of the missionary, the South Sea Islanders constantly engaged in cannibalistic wars that decimated the population. Those wars suddenly ceased with the acceptance of the gospel. In the eighteenth century India was torn with strife caused by the contending European powers. Only one man, Lutheran missionary Christian Schwartz, was trusted and respected by the British, French, and Dutch on the one hand and the Hindu and Muslim leaders on the other. One of the Muslim princes, Hyder Ali, refused to deal directly with the British, saying, "Send me the Christian; he will not deceive me."

And what shall be said of China between 1910 and 1935, when warlords ravaged the countryside? During those years hundreds of missionaries were carried off by bandits. Some were held for ransom, others were killed, and still others died in captivity. Yet in the midst of all the turmoil the missionaries remained at their posts. On at least a half dozen occasions they offered their good services and effected a truce between the various warlords, thus preventing further destruction. In 1923 at the height of the troubles a group of missionaries signed the following declaration:

> The undersigned, American missionaries, are in China as messengers of the gospel of brotherhood and peace.... We therefore express our earnest desire that no form of military pressure ... be exerted to protect us or our property; and that in the event of our capture by lawless persons or our death at their hands, no money be paid for our release, no punitive expeditions be sent out, and no indemnity be exacted.[6]

In more recent years the missionaries have continued their mission of peace. In civil wars in Nigeria, India, Pakistan, Burundi, Vietnam, and other countries they have protected national leaders, political as well as religious, organized and supervised refugee camps, and engaged in relief and rehabilitation. And working alongside the missionaries have been the national Christians, some of whom were themselves refugees.

5. He is a bearer of culture. In some circles this is a debatable subject. Anthropologists especially have been critical of the missionary for "interfering" with the indigenous culture. The missionary has been blamed for many things. Not content with saving their souls, he insisted that they wear clothes, learn English, cut out smoking, drinking, dancing, and carousing. In short, he presumed to change their whole life-style; and this, the anthropologists say, is bad.

First: In reply we would have to say that with or without intention

---

[6] R. Pierce Beaver, *Envoys of Peace* (Grand Rapids: Eerdmans, 1964), p. 29.

the missionary is a bearer of culture. It cannot be otherwise. No matter how hard he tries, he can never completely divest himself of his Western-Christian orientation. Sir James Jeans, leading astronomer in England in the 1930s, wrote a fascinating book, *The Universe Around Us,* in which he said that when a baby throws its rattle on the floor, it disturbs the molecular motion of every star in the universe! The author cannot vouch for the veracity of that statement; but he does know that something similar takes place when a missionary resides for any length of time in a "primitive" culture. Almost by a process of osmosis a transfer of culture takes place. He cannot walk down the street without arousing the curiosity of the populace. They are bound to ask questions, and from his answers they will make certain deductions. Already they are well on their way to being indirectly affected by the new culture that has appeared in their midst. Before long they will visit in his home, and they will be most unusual people if they don't want what they see there. The missionary's problem is not how to talk them into accepting his culture, but how to dissuade them from wanting it in the first place.

Second: It is simply not true that missionaries set out deliberately to change the indigenous culture. There were, of course, some who did this; but they should not be regarded as the norm for missionary behavior. The vast majority of missionaries were interested primarily in spiritual and moral renewal, not in cultural change *per se.*

Third: If the missionary only preaches the gospel and does nothing to help solve the social and economic problems of a backward people, he is accused of being pietistic and interested only in personal salvation. If on the other hand he introduces new tools and time-saving, money-making devices he is accused of interfering with the culture. Either way he is faulted.

Fourth: Is all cultural change bad? If the missionaries did wrong to share the good things of Western civilization with the Africans, the Africans now have their own sovereign, independent states and are free to revert to the kind of indigenous culture they enjoyed before the coming of the missionary. One does not observe any stampede in that direction. In fact, there is plenty of evidence that our friends in the Third World are determined to catch up with the West as fast as they can. At present there are 200,000 of them in Western countries studying our "advanced" civilization with a view to raising their own standards of living. They want all the mechanical gadgets of our technology from Parker pens to Phantom jets.

Fifth: Is the missionary not under obligation to minister to the needs of the whole man? Can he save his soul and refuse to heal his body or inform his mind? Should he leave the people to the tender mercies of the witch doctor or should he make available to them the marvelous discoveries of modern medicine? Is it wrong to teach people to build better and more durable houses, to use better seed and reap a bigger harvest? Is it wrong to eliminate malaria, typhus, yellow fever, and other equally devastating diseases? Is it wrong to teach a child to read?

To ask these questions is to answer them. The missionary made no mistake. He *is* the bearer of culture. He has not only an evangelistic mandate; he has a cultural mandate as well. He *is* his brother's keeper. The good things of life that he enjoys are not really his. They are God's gifts to mankind. It so happens that they occur in greater abundance in the Western world. This does not give us the right to keep them to ourselves. As followers of Jesus Christ we are duty bound to love our neighbors as ourselves (Mt 22:39), and we must love them in deed and in truth, not simply in word or speech (1 Jn 3:18).

If there is any doubt in our minds on this score, we have only to recall the teachings of our Lord, especially the parable of the Good Samaritan (Lk 10). The same emphasis is found in other parts of the New Testament. Paul declares that it is incumbent on Christians to do good to all men (Ga 6:10). The apostle John asks the question: "If any one has the world's goods and sees his brother in need, yet closes his heart against him, how does God's love abide in him?" (1 Jn 3:17).

Sixth: The missionary need not be either defensive or apologetic about being an agent of culture change. He is simply following in the footsteps of the Master.

> The fact is that the greatest cultural transformation in the history of mankind was brought about by a single Missionary, the Divine Legate Himself, Who declared Himself to be nothing less than "the Light of man" (John 1:4) and "the Way, the Truth, and the Life" (John 14:6), Whose mission it was "to cast fire" upon the earth until every tribe and nation, even those in the remotest corners of the earth, would be consumed by that "fire" (Luke 12:49).[7]

How Important Is a Call?

No aspect of the Christian mission is more puzzling than this problem of a call. It is the biggest hang-up that young people have as they face the claims of the mission field. At every panel discussion on missions the questions come thick and fast: "What exactly is a missionary call?" "How can I know that I have a call?" "Can I be

---

[7] Louis J. Luzbetak, *The Church and Cultures* (Techny, IL: Divine Word Publications, 1970), p. 5.

a missionary without a call?" These questions are asked by dedicated Christians who take the Great Commission seriously and genuinely desire to know and do God's will. The questions are fair questions; they deserve honest answers.

In dealing with this most important subject we must avoid two extreme positions. On the one hand there are those who insist that everyone must have what they call a "Macedonian call" such as Paul experienced at Troas (Acts 16:9-10). This is usually thought to be associated with voices, visions, dreams, and other mysterious happenings whereby a clear knowledge of God's will is directly and infallibly imparted to the consciousness of the seeking soul. Without this kind of esoteric experience it is impossible to receive a missionary call. Therefore everyone ought to seek such an experience and wait patiently until it comes.

At the other end of the spectrum are those who maintain that because all Christians are missionaries, no call of any kind is required. Missionary work is not different from any other kind of Christian service. Indeed, there is no essential difference between a missionary and a butcher, or a baker, or a candlestick maker. If you want to be a missionary, hop a plane, go where you like, and do your own thing when you get there. Don't get uptight about such trivial matters as time, call, place, board, ministry, etc. Just hang loose and assume that the Lord will guide.

Needless to say both positions are wrong. Those who advocate the first frequently end up by staying at home. Those who practice the second often do more harm than good on the mission field, and come home with a feeling of failure and frustration. The truth lies somewhere between the two extremes. This leads us to the first question.

IS A CALL NECESSARY?

Much depends on the kind of call one has in mind. The word *call* is used in many different ways in the New Testament. In most instances it refers to Christian life, not service. There is a general call of God (Ro 9:24-26) which became articulate in Christ (Lk 5:32). All believers are called to be saints (Ro 1:7), and the ultimate purpose of such a call is that they might be conformed to the image of Jesus Christ (Ro 8:30). In the meantime *all* believers are called to grace (Ga 1:6), peace (1 Co 7:15), light (1 Pe 2:9), hope (Eph 4:4), glory (1 Th 2:12), holiness (1 Th 4:7), liberty (Ga 5:13), and suffering (1 Pe 2:20-21).

In addition there is a second kind of call—a call to Christian service. This is not addressed to all, but only to those who are called upon to leave their ordinary occupation and devote themselves full time to what Peter called "prayer and the ministry of the Word" (Acts 6:4). All are called to be saints (Ro 1:7); not all are called to be apostles (1 Co 12:29). Paul in his epistles is careful to point out that he was a genuine apostle (1 Co 9). Moreover he insisted that he was an apostle by the will (1 Co 1:1) and calling (Ro 1:1) of God. He did not choose this high calling (1 Co 9:16-18), nor was it conferred on him by others (Ga 1:1).

He was an apostle "by the will of God," and he described himself as having been *made* a minister of the gospel (Eph 3:7). He was *appointed* to be a preacher, apostle, and teacher (2 Ti 1:11). It is true, of course, that he labored with his hands to support himself and his colleagues (Acts 20:34); but he did not regard tent-making as his vocation. He never referred to himself as a "tent-maker by the will of God," though certainly he did not take himself out of the will of God by resorting now and again to his old trade. He *was* an apostle; he made tents simply to pay the bills. And to his dying day Paul could never adequately express his utter amazement at the grace of God that made him a preacher and an apostle (1 Co 15:9-10; 1 Ti 1: 12-14).

The so-called Macedonian call (Acts 16:9-10) wasn't a missionary call at all. Paul had been a missionary for years before that. His call to missionary service coincided with his conversion, when God said to Ananias, "He is a chosen instrument of mine to carry my name before the Gentiles and kings and the sons of Israel" (Acts 9:15). This call was later confirmed by the Holy Spirit when He said to the leaders of the church in Antioch: "Set apart for me Barnabas and Saul for the work to which I have called them" (Acts 13:2).

What then was the nature of the Macedonian call? It was not a divine call at all; it was simply a human call for help. The call came not from God but from a "man of Macedonia." The plea was, "Come over to Macedonia and help us." This episode had nothing whatever to do with a missionary call. It was simply a matter of guidance to a man already in full-time missionary service. Paul had reached the extreme western end of the continent of Asia and had several options open to him. Apparently he had not given any thought to crossing over into Europe. Instead he attempted to turn eastward again, first into the Roman province of Asia and then into Bithynia; but the Holy Spirit prevented him in both instances. Where should he go? Obviously he was in need of special guidance if he were to take the gospel for the first time into Europe. The decision he was about to make was of such momentous importance that he required unusual guidance. This God gave him in the vision of the man from Macedonia. It is a great pity that this so-called Macedonian call should ever have been equated with a missionary call.

The term *missionary call* should never have been coined. It is not Scriptural and therefore can be harmful. Thousands of youth desiring to serve the Lord have waited and waited for some mysterious "missionary call" that never came. After a time they became weary in waiting and gave up the idea of going to the mission field.

Does this mean that there is no such thing as a call of any kind? No, indeed. There is a call, a very definite call, to the service of God on a full-time basis. Jesus "called" Peter and Andrew to follow Him. "Immediately they left their nets and followed him" (Mt 4:20). Later He "called" James and John. "Immediately they left the boat and their father, and followed him" (Mt 4:22). When Luke describes the same event, he says: "And when they had brought their boats to land, *they left everything* and followed him" (Lk 5:11).

It seems clear from this passage that this "call" involved a clean break with their previous occupation and launched them into a brand new occupation, that of "fishers of men." Apparently it was not possible for them to be fishers of fish and fishers of men at the same time. This does not mean that there was anything wrong with their previous occupation or that their new occupation was to be regarded as "higher" or "holier." It was a completely different occupation that would require all their time and energy. In present-day parlance it would be "full-time Christian service." It is worth noting that these four men and the other apostles never went back to their old occupations.

This idea of a call to Christian service is further strengthened by our Lord's attitude toward those who took it upon themselves to volunteer for His service. One fellow in a moment of enthusiasm said, "I will follow you wherever you go." Jesus replied: "Foxes have holes, and birds of the air have nests; but the Son of man has nowhere to lay his head" (Lk 9:57-58). Apparently the man withdrew his offer at that point.

Another person volunteered, "I will follow you, Lord; but let me first say farewell to those at home." Jesus replied: "No one who puts his hand to the plow and looks back is fit for the kingdom of God" (Lk 9:61-62).

There are those who object to the terms *secular* and *sacred* as applied to the vocational life of the Christian. To the dedicated Christian, they say, all vocations are sacred because whatever he does, he does it unto the Lord (Co 3:23). This, of course, is true. It does not, however, invalidate the distinction that the New Testament seems to make between secular and sacred ministries.

In several passages of his epistles Paul seems to make a distinction between the "spiritual" and the "secular" or "material" (Ro 15:27; 1 Co 9:11). In his own case Paul was conscious of having been appointed to a special ministry (1 Ti 1:12), that of teaching and preaching the Word (2 Ti 1:11). Moreover, he recognized the possibility that he might fail in the ministry (1 Co 9:27) and expressed the hope that he would be able to complete it (Acts 20:24), which he seems to have done (2 Ti 4:7).

He spoke of Epaphras as a "faithful minister of Christ" (Co 1:7; 4:12), a description he obviously did not apply to everyone. He reminded Timothy of his consecration to the gospel ministry when the elders laid their hands on him (1 Ti 4:14). There is nothing in the New Testament to suggest that men in secular employment were ever set apart to their work by the laying on of hands. This seems to have been reserved for those whose lifework was directly connected with the preaching of the gospel and the life of the church.

Apparently the apostles felt that there was something "sacred" or "special" about their ministry, for when the daily distribution of food threatened the unity of the church in Jerusalem, they refused to get involved in "serving tables." They said, "It is not right that we should give up preaching the word of God to serve tables" (Acts 6:2). Instead they decided that they would continue to devote themselves to "prayer and to the ministry of the word."

It is difficult to escape the conviction that the early church regarded "prayer and the ministry of the word" as being the equivalent of what we now call "full-time Christian service." All Christians are expected to work and witness for Christ regardless of their vocation; but only a few are called to leave everything and follow Christ in order to give themselves unreservedly to prayer and the ministry of the Word. It is important to preserve this distinction in a day when egalitarianism threatens to do away with *all* distinctions between the clergy and the laity in the Christian church.

WHAT CONSTITUTES A CALL TO CHRISTIAN SERVICE?

The call to Christian service seldom comes as a meteor out of the blue. More often it is a growing conviction based on certain well-defined principles laid down in the Word of God. As one walks with the Lord in the light of His Word, he discovers that step by step he is led to the place where he hears the still small voice behind him saying, "This is the way, walk in it" (Is 30:21).

1. **Acknowledgment of the claims of Christ.** The very first step in the process is the recognition of the Lordship of Christ. "Jesus Christ is Lord," was the great affirmation of the early church. That one great fact ought to settle everything. He created me for His glory.

He redeemed me with His blood. He saved me by His grace. He keeps me by His power. Therefore He has first claim on my life. I am His personal property. Body, mind, and soul I belong to Him. He has the right to do with me exactly what He likes. I am His obedient servant. When He speaks, I listen. When He calls, I answer. When He commands, I obey. I have only one pertinent question to ask of Him: "Lord, what wilt Thou have me to do?" If He wants me in Christian service, I have no option but to obey.

2. **Understanding of the will of God.** God's will is twofold, general and specific. His general will embraces His plan and purpose for the whole creation. This is spelled out in broad outlines in the Scriptures. There is no mystery about it. It is plain for all to see. For instance, we know that God is not willing that any should perish, but that all should come to repentance (2 Pe 3:9). When we pray for the salvation of our loved ones and add, "If it be Thy will," we weaken our prayer. God has already told us that it *is* His will. With regard to His own children, we know that it is His will that *all* of them should be holy in character and conduct (1 Th 4:3). There can be no doubt about this.

In addition God has His specific will which differs with each individual Christian. "We are his workmanship, created in Christ Jesus for good works, which God prepared beforehand, that we should walk in them" (Eph 2:10). God has a tailor-made plan for the life of every believer. The details, of course, are not spelled out in the Scriptures. To ascertain the specific will of God the mind of the believer must be renewed day by day by an act of continual consecration (Ro 12:1-2). When discovered, that will proves to be "good and acceptable and perfect."

It is not easy to ascertain God's specific will. It takes time and discipline. Moreover, it is impossible to know God's specific will unless we are willing to bring our lives into conformity with His general will. Only when we do His general will, which we know, will He give us light regarding His specific will, which we don't know. It is at this point that many Christians go wrong. They pay little attention to what God has revealed regarding His general will, but spend much time and thought trying to ascertain His specific will.

3. **Susceptibility to the leading of the Holy Spirit.** What constitutes a call to Christian service? It is easier to ask that question than to answer it. Indeed, it is probably impossible to answer it to the satisfaction of everyone, for the simple reason that the call is communicated to the soul by the Holy Spirit, who works in different ways with different people. Speaking of the regenerating work of the Holy

Spirit Jesus said, "The wind blows where it wills, and you hear the sound of it, but you do not know whence it comes or whither it goes; so is everyone who is born of the Spirit" (Jn 3:8). The same element of mystery accompanies the consecrating work of the Holy Spirit. He works, moves, directs, and controls in His own sovereign way, and no one can be sure just when, where, or what His next move will be. For this reason it is dangerous to compare one Christian's experience with another's.

No two Christians are alike either in their conversion experience or in the matter of guidance that comes later. The Holy Spirit deals with each believer in a manner best suited to his needs and interests, his attitudes and aptitudes. It is therefore difficult to tell another person how the Holy Spirit is likely to lead him.

To most serious-minded Christians Jesus Christ is a "living, bright reality." Not so the Holy Spirit. He seems to be so distant, so ethereal, so unreal that many Christians aren't even on speaking terms with Him. John E. Skoglund calls Him "the missing person."[8] Indeed, that is precisely what He is to many Christians. Some of them would have to confess with the believers in Ephesus: "We have never even heard that there is a Holy Spirit" (Acts 19:2).

To the early church the Holy Spirit was not simply a power to be employed but a person to be loved, trusted, consulted, and obeyed. When the first church council wrote up its final report it said: "It has seemed good to the Holy Spirit and to us" (Acts 15:28). Imagine any church council talking that way today!

The Holy Spirit was as real to the early church as Jesus was to His disciples in the days of His flesh. He was indeed the "other Comforter" sent to take the place of the risen, ascended Lord (Jn 14:16). The early Christians had little difficulty in getting guidance. They lived on such a high spiritual plane that communion with the Holy Spirit was a matter of course. They confided in Him and He spoke to them. Their ears were attuned to the sound of His voice. When He spoke they listened and obeyed. One problem with present-day Christians is that we have failed to develop our spiritual faculties. We are so busy running here and there to get counsel and advice from pastors, teachers, and guidance counselors that we have neglected to listen for the still, small voice of the Holy Spirit. He speaks, but we are not listening. And all the while we wonder why we don't get a call to Christian service.

4. Confirmation by the local church. This is an aspect of the call to Christian service that is prominent in the New Testament but is

---

8 John E. Skoglund, *To the Whole Creation* (Valley Forge: Judson Press, 1962), chap. 5.

almost completely missing in church life today. The classic example is the command of the Holy Spirit to the church in Antioch: "Set apart for me Barnabas and Saul for the work to which I have called them" (Acts 13:2). If the Holy Spirit has already called them, is that not enough? Why does the church have to get in on the act?

The reason is that the church is the pillar and ground of the truth (1 Ti 3:15). It is the channel through which God's saving grace flows out to a needy world (Acts 1:8). The evangelization of the world is not the work of a few individuals but the responsibility of the church as a whole. Paul and Barnabas were sent out by the Holy Spirit *and* the local church, and when they returned they made their report to that church.

All of Paul's co-workers mentioned in the Acts of the Apostles were identified with local churches. Timothy was "well spoken of by the brethren at Lystra and Iconium" (Acts 16:2). Epaphras hailed from Colosse (Co 1:7), Gaius from Derbe, and Sopater from Berea (Acts 20:4). When the fledgling church in Antioch was just getting under way, the church in Jerusalem sent Barnabas to help the believers there to get established (Acts 11:22). In the early church there were no "independent" missionaries. Each one was a member of a local church, approved by that church, and sent forth and supported by that church.

The call to Christian service can come only from the Holy Spirit, but there should be some kind of confirmation on the part of the local church of which the individual is a member. That church will know him best, and if its leadership is what it ought to be it will be in a position to give its blessing to those going into full-time Christian service. If this were done it would greatly strengthen the hands and encourage the hearts of young candidates for the Christian ministry. It would help to confirm the leading of the Lord given directly to the person himself.

CALL VERSUS GUIDANCE

A clear distinction must be made between a call to full-time Christian service and guidance. We have already stated that the "Macedonian call" in Acts 16 was not a missionary call at all, but simply a matter of guidance. The call comes once in a lifetime; and once it is understood and obeyed, it need not be repeated. But guidance is something that is required throughout the whole of life.

Where does the Lord want His servant to serve? At home or overseas? He can't be in both places at the same time, so guidance is needed. And even when he knows he will be serving overseas, he still needs guidance regarding the country to which he will go and the mission under which he will serve. These important considerations are not left to chance or even to the choice of the individual. God deploys His servants according to His own wisdom. He sent Paul to the Gentiles and Peter to the Jews (Ga 2:7-8). He directed William Carey to India, David Livingstone to Africa, and Hudson Taylor to China.

The missionary is not the only one who needs guidance. Those who serve at home need it just as much. Does the Christian worker become a pastor, an evangelist, or a Christian education director? Or should he teach in a Bible college or seminary? And if he goes into the pastorate, where will he minister? In Maine or California or Colorado? And how long will he remain in any one church? Five years? Ten years? Or thirty years? In all these momentous decisions the Christian worker is dependent on God for guidance. But this kind of guidance should not be mistaken for a call.

HOW DOES ONE RECEIVE
A CALL TO CHRISTIAN SERVICE?

God is sovereign in His choice of the servants who will serve Him. This does not mean that we sit down with folded hands and wait for some miraculous event to catapult us into the service of Jesus Christ. There must be on our part an attitude of receptivity and readiness so that when the call comes we will be in a position to hear and answer. The chances of our getting a call will be greatly enhanced if we meet certain conditions. Among these are the following:

1. **An open mind.** Everybody prides himself on having an open mind but few actually achieve it. Man's capacity for self-deception is enormous. We think we have an open mind while all along we are victims of our own prejudices and predilections. We have long ago decided that there are certain things we will not do. We wouldn't dare say it to God; but in our own minds we have decided, "Anything but Christian service," or "Anywhere but the foreign field." So long as we harbor preconceived negative notions about the will of God or the work of the church we shall wait in vain for a call.

It is incumbent on every young Christian to be absolutely honest in his dealings with God, to keep his options open, to allow the Holy Spirit to take full control of his mental faculties. This is by no means easy. In fact it is a never-ending battle. J. B. Phillips expresses it well: "Our battle is to bring down every deceptive fantasy and every imposing defense that men erect against the true knowledge of God. We even fight to capture every thought until it acknowledges the authority of Christ" (2 Co 10:5).

2. An attentive ear. An open mind is a great achievement, but it may still fall short unless it is accompanied by an attentive ear. It is not enough to rid one's mind of all "deceptive fantasies." We must also have our ear open to the voice of the Holy Spirit.

We know all too well that the hearing faculty can be turned on or off almost at will. It doesn't take much practice to sharpen one's sense of hearing provided there is sufficient motivation. In the dead of night the young mother can hear the cry of her firstborn son and is instantly on her feet to prepare the two o'clock feeding, while the father in the same room sleeps blissfully through the entire operation. What makes the difference? Do not both parents have the same hearing faculty? The maternal instinct in one parent sharpened her sense of hearing to the point where the slightest cry from the little one in the crib brought her out of bed. She slept, as we say, with "one ear open" while her husband slept with both ears closed.

The same thing can happen in the spiritual realm. With a little practice we can train ourselves to detect the slightest whisper of the Holy Spirit when He speaks to us. On the other hand we can turn a deaf ear to His entreaties. We need do this only two or three times and our hearing faculty will be so impaired that we will be beyond the reach of His voice.

Christians have been known to complain: "How is it that God speaks to others, but never to me?" It may be that God did speak, not once but many times, but they were not listening. Effective communication is possible only when the speaker and the listener are in direct contact. If only one is operating there can be no communication.

3. A pure heart. Understanding God's truth, or ascertaining God's will, is not a purely intellectual exercise. It has a moral dimension to it. God does not reveal Himself to every Tom, Dick, or Harry whose interest in His truth takes the form of intellectual curiosity. God reveals His truth not to those who want to *know* it but to those who are prepared to *do* it. The Jews of Jesus' day had difficulty in deciding the true origin of His teaching, whether it was from God or from man. Jesus said to them, "If any man's will is to *do* his [God's] will, he shall know whether the teaching is from God or whether I am speaking on my own authority" (Jn 7:17).

In the Hall of Science at the Century of Progress World's Fair in Chicago in 1933-34 there was a huge motto which read: "Nature reveals her secrets only to those who obey her laws." Every scientist knows the truth of those words. This truth, however, is not confined to the physical realm of science. It is likewise true in the metaphysical realm of theology. God reveals His truths only to those who obey His laws. One of His laws is that since He is holy (Ps 99:5) all who wish to have fellowship with Him must likewise be holy (He 12:14). King David asked: "Who shall ascend the hill of the Lord? And who shall stand in his holy place?" And the answer came back: "He who has clean hands and a pure heart, who does not lift up his soul to what is false, and does not swear deceitfully" (Ps 24:3-4). A pure heart is absolutely essential to communication between God and man—in either direction. The psalmist said: "If I had cherished iniquity in my heart, the Lord would not have listened" (Ps 66:18).

The person with unconfessed sin in his life will wait in vain for any call from the Lord, other than the call to repent (Is 55:7). For the Christian waiting for God's call it is not enough to have an open mind and an attentive ear; he must also have a pure heart, for only the pure in heart will ever see God (Mt 5:8).

4. Busy hands. There is a common saying that Satan is sure to find some work for idle hands to do. Doubtless there is some truth in the statement. If Satan prefers idle hands, God certaintly does not. If the Scriptures are anything to go by, God's call comes to those who are busy, not idle. Moses, David, Peter, Matthew, and Paul were all engaged in some demanding work when the call of God came. He wants workers, not loafers, in His vineyard. Jesus Himself was the great Worker. He said, "My Father is working still, and I am working" (Jn 5:17). Again He said, "We must work the works of him who sent me while it is day; night comes when no man can work" (Jn 9:4).

Any person contemplating even the possibility of a call should begin by getting involved in some kind of work for the Lord. How is God going to call a person into full-time service if that person has never engaged in any kind of Christian work? One could begin by teaching a Sunday school class, or engaging in open-air work, or home visitation, or tract distribution, or rescue mission work, or leading a youth group, or helping in a vacation Bible school, or doing any one of the many things that need to be done in the local church.

In this connection it is instructive to observe that the vast majority of missionary candidates come from the Bible colleges, not from the Christian liberal arts colleges or the secular universities. Why is this? Doubtless the most important reason is that the Bible colleges require all students to engage in practical Christian work during their four years in college. During that time they gain courage, experience, and expertise. As a result they acquire a taste for Christian service, which they might never have done under different circumstances.

It is tragically possible for a student to spend four years in a Christian liberal arts college and never accept a single Christian service assignment, or attend a single missionary prayer meeting, or read a single missionary biography or periodical, or talk personally with a visiting chapel speaker, or even give his testimony in a class meeting. It is fair to ask: How is the Holy Spirit to reach that student with a call to Christian service?

5. Ready feet. The psalmist said: "I will run in the way of thy commandments" (Ps 119:32). Isaiah said: "How beautiful on the mountains are the feet of him who brings good tidings, who publishes peace" (Is 52:7). The time is short (1 Co 7:29) and the king's business requires haste (1 Sa 21:8). Indecision and procrastination have more than once played havoc with a call to Christian service.

Young people facing Christian service encounter two temptations. One is to run before the Lord; the other is to lag behind; for every one who succumbs to the first temptation there are ten who fall before the second. There are people who can't bring themselves to make a major decision such as that required to enter full-time Christian service. They examine all aspects of the situation; they pray about the matter; they discuss it with others; they do everything but come to a conclusion.

One problem is that they don't understand the true nature of divine guidance; consequently they are not prepared to step out in faith. They want to wait until their guidance is 100 percent certain; and that, of course, never happens. Guidance as granted by God is always perfect; but once it has filtered through the human mind it is no longer perfect. If one waits until he is *absolutely* sure of the Lord's leading, he will wait forever. Divine guidance is never 100 percent certain; if it were, where would faith come in? We must remember that the Christian walks by faith and not by sight (2 Co 5:7); which means that he must be willing to act on the guidance God has given and expect Him to be responsible for all the consequences that flow from his obedience.

Even Paul, when giving instructions regarding Christian marriage, was obliged to say, "I *think* that I have the Spirit of God" (1 Co 7:40). And after he received the so-called Macedonian call, Luke says, "Immediately we sought to go into Macedonia, *concluding* that God had called us to preach the gospel to them" (Acts 16:10).

Somewhere along the line the individual must make up his mind to act, to get going. It is always easier to steer a moving vehicle than a stationary one. Some would-be missionaries give the impression that they are waiting for God to pack their trunks, buy their tickets, and see them off at the airport.

2

The Measure of the Man

In North America there are almost five hundred missionary agencies involved in overseas operations. A small number of these occupy a supportive role and do little more than collect and distribute mission funds. The overwhelming majority are sending agencies that require both men and money.

Recruitment is a perennial problem with the sending agencies. To begin with, all missions have their share of dropouts. Although these are not as numerous as generally assumed, they do pose a problem. The average dropout rate is about 2.5 percent per year. The membership of the older missions is further depleted each year by two additional factors, deaths and retirements. Taken together these three factors represent an annual attrition rate of about 10 percent. This means that a large mission with eight hundred members requires eighty new missionaries every year just to maintain its existing work. If expansion is contemplated, additional recruits will be needed.

Recruitment is a long and costly process, especially for the interdenominational missions that do not have their own denomination on which they can rely for recruits. The candidate secretary has to visit ten or twenty colleges each year, speak in chapel, interview interested students, write follow-up letters, prepare literature, conduct seminars, process application papers, and finally make arrangements for candidate school in June. Very few missions are getting recruits in sufficient numbers to permit them to expand their program. If they manage to hold their own they are doing well. If it were not for the short-term missionaries the situation would be critical indeed. The short-terms-abroad program has become so popular that in some missions half the new missionaries going out each year are short-termers.

.Most of the missions are now accepting short-term workers, who spend anywhere from one to three years overseas. This new program adds enormously to the burdens of recruitment, for it takes just as long to process the application of a short-termer as it does that of a career missionary. In the initial stages the new program works well; but after five or ten years the homebound traffic gets rather heavy. Instead of having to replace only 10 percent of the membership each year, it will become necessary to raise that to 20 percent.

If this trend continues the missions will have to devote more time and money to the task of recruitment.

Hang-ups Regarding Missionary Life

Of all the forms of Christian service the missionary vocation seems to inspire the greatest fear. Many a dedicated Christian has said in his heart, "I am willing, Lord, to be anything but a missionary." Somehow missionary work seems to be so difficult and so demanding that only the most courageous souls are willing to join up.

Missionary work, like many other things in life, looks more forbidding at a distance than it does close up. The hill that appears to be very steep from a distance has a way of flattening out as one approaches it. There are very few missionaries who would not have to confess that in the beginning of their career they had misgivings of one kind or another; but as they got into the work they discovered to their surprise that one by one the misgivings disappeared.

In this section we shall discuss only the more prominent hang-ups that trouble Christian youth today. These hang-ups, it should be noted, loom much larger for the career missionary than for the short-termer. One can endure almost anything if he knows beforehand it will last for only a year or two. One reason for the popularity of the Peace Corps is the fact that the term of service is only twenty-one months and then it's all over; but the volunteer has the satisfaction of knowing that he devoted two good years to helping others.

1. **Unconditional surrender.** The very phrase scares some people. The word *surrender* has a rather unfortunate connotation. For most people it carries with it the idea of conflict, crisis, and capitulation leading to permanent subjugation. Paul Little has suggested that we drop the word altogether and speak of *affirming*, rather than surrender-

ing to, the will of God. He may have a point. And the adjective *unconditional* makes the idea more horrendous still.

The New Testament makes it clear that Jesus Christ is Lord and His Lordship extends to all of life. Either He is Lord of all or He isn't Lord at all. He won't play second fiddle to anyone. He even went so far as to say, "He who loves father or mother more than me is not worthy of me; and he who loves son or daughter more than me is not worthy of me" (Mt 10:37). In the New Testament we find the two words *master* and *servant* used in juxtaposition and the combination scares some people. These two words don't sit too well with modern man. They seem to be outmoded ideas.

The real question, however, is not semantic but spiritual. It has its roots in a false concept of the character of God. People seem to have the idea that God is a tyrant who takes sinister delight in inflicting His will on His children. He is just waiting for them to surrender. Then He will move in with all the power at His command, break their wills, destroy their plans, and forever crush their hopes beneath His feet; and for the rest of their days they will be required to grovel in the dust. They have a sneaking suspicion that they can't be a follower of Christ and have fun at the same time. If they once allow God to put them into a strait jacket, they will be doomed to a life of perpetual frustration.

That is one of the greatest lies ever perpetrated by the devil. He has succeeded in getting millions of Christians to believe that lie; and the result has been catastrophic, both for the individuals concerned and for the church as a whole.

It is true that Jesus spoke of self-denial, but *only as a way to self-fulfillment*. He said, "He who finds his life will lose it, and he who loses his life for my sake will find it" (Mt 10:39). Modern man, aided and abetted by the insights of psychology, is striving with all his might and main to achieve self-fulfillment; but he is going about it in the wrong way. He is seeking it directly and for its own sake; and it continues to elude him. For the Christian the way to self-fulfillment is by way of self-denial. This is one of the many paradoxes of the Christian life.

Far from being a tyrant, God is a loving heavenly Father. His lovingkindness is better than life; and His tender mercies are over all His works. Nothing is too great for His power; nothing is too small for His love. He desires our highest good; and to this end He plans for us in love. He would no more crush our hopes than an earthly father would crush the hopes of his children.

He knows all about our training and our talents. He knows us better than we know ourselves. He knows that we function best when we are well adjusted, not maladjusted. Certainly He doesn't have less compassion or less common sense than we do. It would hardly serve His purpose to have us end up as square pegs in round holes.

The most miserable person alive is not the sinner enjoying the pleasures of sin, but the child of God who is trying desperately to serve two masters. There is nothing in the world more frustrating. For the Christian there is only one road to self-fulfillment and that is by way of self-denial. His yoke *is* easy; His burden *is* light (Mt 11:30). His ways are ways of pleasantness and all His paths are peace (Pr 3:17). God's will is good, acceptable, and perfect (Ro 12:2). Samuel Rutherford said, "What a beautiful yoke are youth and grace, Christ and a young man." No man who followed Christ ever lived to regret his decision. Call it "unconditional surrender," or just "plain obedience," or anything you wish; it doesn't make much difference. To follow Christ is to walk in light (Jn 8:12).

2. **Loss of personal freedom.** We in the Western world are living in a period of unprecedented personal freedom. Today's youngsters don't want anybody—including their parents—to tell them what to do. And it all begins at an early age. The four-year-old boy accompanies his mother to the supermarket where he is allowed to choose one of twenty-nine kinds of cereal or one of fifty-seven varieties of cookies. When he gets home he may change his mind and refuse to eat them, in which case he will be given a second choice the following week. In this way he never learns to accept discipline, to knuckle down to authority, or to take "no" for an answer. After twenty-five years of this kind of treatment the young man can be forgiven if he has serious misgivings about joining a mission.

Today's youth are wary of anything belonging to the establishment. Missions, being part of the establishment, come in for their share of distrust. They are reputed to be conservative, paternalistic, even reactionary. They are accused of thinking in old categories and being unwilling to change with the changing times. They cling tenaciously to the outmoded principles and practices of the past and refuse to experiment with new methods and policies. Consequently the youth are turned off.

Mission boards are part of the establishment, all right; and most of the mission executives, through no fault of their own, are on the wrong side of thirty; but that does not mean that they are necessarily inflexible. The mission leaders with whom the author is acquainted are among the most progressive men in Christian service today. They are anything but inflexible. They are conservative in their theology but not in their methodology. Because they are committed to progress, they are open to change. With few exceptions they are aggressive, innovative, and dynamic. They don't pretend to have all the answers. They are just as eager to listen and learn as they are to speak and act. They welcome suggestions from all and sundry, including recent recruits.

A former student of mine spent a year in Japan as a short-term worker. He was amazed when he attended his first prayer meeting to hear a mission leader pray, "Lord, if we're doing anything wrong, show us, and we'll set it right." He soon discovered to his delight that this was the prevailing mood among the missionaries in Japan.

This is not to suggest that every missionary is a law unto himself and does that which is right in his own eyes. Every mission has its principles and practices which have developed over a long period of time. Policies hammered out on the anvil of experience are usually both sound and sane and in time will commend themselves to the new recruit. But there is nothing particularly sacred about such policies. They can be altered. Indeed they are altered from time to time. Most missions hold a top-level consultation at least once every five years, when anything and everything comes under review. Outmoded policies are discarded. New and innovative ideas are discussed and, if found to be workable, adopted.

As for the individual within a mission, it is fair to say that the missionary on the field has at least as much, maybe more, personal freedom than the pastor at home. He is expected to be in sympathy with the aims and policies of the mission, or he wouldn't have joined in the first place; but he is not placed in a strait jacket. There is an honest effort to reconcile group guidance with personal guidance; and if a worker is genuinely unhappy with his assignment, every effort will be made to accommodate him. If necessary he will be transferred to another city or another institution, or assigned to another kind of work. No one is required to remain at the same job year after year if he really believes he is out of the will of God.

It is interesting in this respect to learn that the missionary has much more freedom than does the Peace Corps volunteer. In the Peace Corps it is virtually impossible to have one's assignment changed. This is a source of great frustration.

3. **Raising one's own support.** The mainline denominations have a unified budget which takes care of all their missionaries; consequently no one is expected to raise his own support. Among the smaller, conservative missions, both denominational and interdenominational, the practice is for each recruit to raise his own support before proceeding to the field. Exceptions to this rule include the Christian and Missionary Alliance, Overseas Missionary Fellowship, and maybe one or two others. This policy of raising one's own support is a major hang-up with a growing number of potential missionaries.

They can't bear the thought of going from church to church, cup in hand like a mendicant, "begging" for support. It is embarrassing for the churches and humiliating for the candidates. At least this is what many people think. What are the facts?

It should be acknowledged that for many people this is a real hurdle that they are not sure they can clear. Some people by temperament find it distasteful to ask for help of any kind. They detest asking for money. Somehow it goes against the grain.

Raising support can be a long, tedious, discouraging pursuit, depending on the candidate's background and connections, his personality and speaking ability, the reputation of his mission, and the kind of work into which he is going.

There are just so many evangelical, missionary-minded churches to which the candidates can appeal. Many of them are fully committed already and cannot find room in their budget for another missionary. Not every church will give him a hearing; and not all churches in which he speaks will take on his support. Some won't even give him an offering to defray his expenses.

Raising one's support is costly in time and money. It may take twelve or eighteen months to complete the job. In the process it may be necessary to travel thousands of miles to reach the churches. During all this time where does he live and how does he support himself? If he is married and has a family his problems are compounded.

Some missionary candidates—not many—never succeed in raising their full support. After many months of fruitless effort they become discouraged and give up. They conclude that the mission field is not for them. This is not necessarily a bad thing. It may be God's way of indicating His will. In all his long experience the author has known only three persons in this category, and in each case there was a valid reason for the failure.

What shall be said about the positive side?

The vast majority of candidates succeed in raising their support without much trouble. Some complete the task in a matter of weeks; others take considerably longer. The important thing is that they make the grade.

Almost to a man those who succeed testify that the experience is enriching and rewarding from every point of view. They learn lessons of faith; they get answers to prayer; they have opportunities for witness they never dreamed of. When the ordeal is over they are better and stronger Christians.

In addition to raising their support, they make friends and acquire prayer partners who will stand by them for all the days to come. They may end up with two or three hundred names for their prayer letter list. This kind of support is as important as financial backing.

Contrary to popular opinion the candidate is not entirely on his own, nor does he have to start from scratch. Most of the larger missions have a candidate secretary who is responsible to help the candidate secure his support in the shortest time. The mission will not only stand behind him, it will go before him—writing letters of introduction, contacting pastors, arranging meetings, providing literature, slides, and other helps. Some of the larger churches take on the support of one or two new missionaries each year. To do this they usually get in touch with various mission boards asking for the names of prospective missionaries. In this way some candidates pick up half their support in one church.

There is no reason why the candidate should be embarrassed to make his needs known. When he does so he is on solid Biblical grounds. Moreover, he confers a privilege on the church when he makes it possible for its members to contribute to his support. The churches need to be constantly reminded of the word of our Lord: "It is more blessed to give than to receive" (Acts 20:35). When church members give to the support of a missionary they are laying up treasure in heaven. What they spend on themselves is lost forever.

One important aspect of deputation work that is often overlooked is the ministry the candidate has to the churches he visits. He goes to give as well as to get. It is always thrilling to see a young person in the glow of his first love preparing to go to the mission field. His testimony is bound to make an impression on the audience, especially any young people who may be present.

4. Inadequate financial remuneration. It is common knowledge that missionaries are among the lowest paid people in the world. Their support level is considerably lower than the income of a middle-class American family. What's worse, they don't always get their full support. Consequently they have to "live by faith," with a little help from the "missionary barrel."

Such a prospect is frightening to American youth who have been brought up in the lap of luxury and have been able to acquire anything their hearts desired. Money is no problem. Either they have their own or they can "borrow" from their parents. Teen-age America now has billions of dollars at its disposal annually, and it has created a subculture of its own. And the older generation is no better. They too are interested in shorter hours, longer vacations, and higher salaries. Compared with affluent Americans the missionary appears to be poverty-stricken.

Another unattractive feature is the practice of giving all missionaries the same allowance regardless of their position in the mission or their years of experience. There are those who advocate that this policy of equal remuneration for all should be abolished. Every missionary, they say, should be paid what he is worth. Only when such incentives are provided will we get the caliber of missionary we want.

Not many people are aware of the significant progress that has been made along these lines in recent years. In the first place it should be noted that the missionaries are better cared for than ever before. They will never get rich on what they are making, but their allowance permits them to live quite comfortably *in the society in which they reside.* To say that a missionary to India gets only two thousand dollars a year sounds incredibly low; but when it is remembered that the average per capita annual income in India is not much more than one hundred dollars, the picture changes drastically. It *is* possible for a single person to live comfortably in India on two thousand dollars a year.

This is not to say that the missionary on the foreign field enjoys all the amenities that go to make up the American way of life. Nor is it desirable that he should. His standard of living may be low by American standards, but in most cases it is high by the standards of the host country.

The missionary must be prepared to live the incarnational life and get as close to the people as possible; only then is he following in the footsteps of the Master who, though He was rich, for our sakes became poor that we through His poverty might be rich (2 Co 8:9). He warned us that a man's life does not consist in the abundance of things that he possesses (Lk 12:15).

It is difficult for the American Christian, accustomed as he is to his affluence, to take Jesus seriously. It is amazing what people can get along without and be happy. After only two years in China the author and his wife lost all their earthly goods and chattels in one day—thanks to the Japanese air force. They remained in China for another seven years without their possessions and never missed them. There are two ways in which a person may be rich. One is in the multiplicity of his possessions. The other is in the simplicity of his wants. Madison Avenue has brainwashed the American people, including not a few Christians, into believing that modern man cannot be happy without the toys and trinkets produced by a technological civilization. If nobody else is prepared to explode the myth surely the missionary should be.

5. Separation from children. This is the greatest single hang-up, especially for young mothers. They cannot bring themselves to contemplate the possibility of sending their children off to boarding school at the tender age of six or seven, after which they will see them only once or twice a year for short vacation periods. It seems to be so unnatural and unnecessary. Moreover, they have been led to believe that MKs have warped personalities and are not a very good advertisement for the gospel or the missionary vocation. Besides, one's first responsibility is to one's own family, not to the church, or the world, or even the work.

Having been through the experience of parting with his own two boys when they both went away to school at the same time, the author has no desire to deny the magnitude of this problem. It was the only thing he and his wife ever did in fifteen years in China that they thought of as a sacrifice. Having said that, it is necessary to place the problem in proper perspective.

To begin with, we must go back to the Scriptures and discover what Christ had to say about the matter. Few of His statements are stronger or clearer than His statement on family ties. "He who loves father or mother more than me is not worthy of me; and he who loves son or daughter more than me is not worthy of me" (Mt 10:37). However difficult it is to work it out in practice, we are forced to confess that all horizontal relationships must be subservient to the vertical relationship between Christ and the disciple. Nobody, not even the dearest person on earth, must be allowed to come between the disciple and his Lord. Jesus Christ must have first place in our affections as well as in everything else. Otherwise the Lordship of Christ is a meaningless cliché. This does not mean that we abandon our children or repudiate our parents (1 Ti 5:8); but it does mean that *in principle* we recognize the supremacy of Jesus Christ in *all* relationships of life.

Some missions permit the parents to choose for themselves how and where their children will be educated; others require the children to attend the mission school. The separation is not nearly so traumatic as some people imagine, either for the parents or for the children. If the children have been psychologically prepared for the event they may actually look forward to going to school. They not only survive; they enjoy life in school. In fact, the act of separation is usually harder on the parents than on the children.

Once the child makes the initial adjustment, which usually takes only a few days, he settles down to a life of comfort and contentment. He has other children of his own age, language, and culture with whom he can study and play. Classes are small enough to permit individual tutoring where necessary. Teachers are dedicated as well as competent. Homework is done together under supervision, which means that no one falls behind. And best of all—there is no television!

Houseparents are in charge of the dormitories and give themselves unstintingly to the children under their care. Each school has an infirmary with a registered nurse on call twenty-four hours around the clock. The larger schools have their own doctor on the staff. Everything possible is done to provide the children with a home away from home. It is no exaggeration to say that the MKs in a mission school are given more attention and security than the children in American suburbia.

There are several advantages to communal life. Discipline is no problem when it is applied across the board and everyone is doing the same thing at the same time. Children reared in that environment are apt to be less possessive, for they must share their things with others; they are more self-reliant, for they must make their own beds, clean their own rooms, and be responsible for their share of the daily chores. The author had two sons reared in China and one in the United States. He has no doubts about the relative merits of the two systems.

Schools for missionaries' children are not penal institutions nor are they reformatories. They are a combination of home, school, and church where the prevailing atmosphere is surcharged with Christian love. There is no need to shed any tears for the MKs on the mission field. They should be reserved for the "underprivileged" kids at home.

6. The lot of the single woman. Every woman, sometime in her life, entertains the hope of getting married and raising a family. This is her God-given right and privilege. Paul tells us that the man is not independent of the woman, nor the woman of the man (1 Co 11:11). They were made for each other and, other things being equal, function better as man and wife than as separate individuals. And this includes a great deal more than sex.

In the missionary body the women outnumber the men three to two, which means that one out of every three women missionaries is doomed to single blessedness for the rest of her life. Such a prospect can hardly be pleasing to the woman who goes out single. Her chances of getting married after she gets to the field are rather slim. With some women the desire to have a family is so strong that it overrides every other consideration. For all such persons the thought of going to the mission field single is horrendous. Single blessedness is not for everyone. Jesus said as much in Matthew 19:12. So did Paul in 1 Corinthians 7:9. No one should be criticized for leaving missionary service to get married. This is a matter between the individual and God. One missionary, after a frustrating term of service in Africa, came home on furlough vowing that she would not return to the field without a husband. She meant business, for when she failed to get a husband she refused to go back. Later on she achieved her ambition. She married a widower with three children and today is a pastor's wife and very happy. Who is to say that she did wrong— either in going to the field the first time or in refusing to go the second time? The final judgment in all such cases must rest with the Lord (1 Co 4:5).

On the other hand let no one jump to the conclusion that the single women on the mission field are pining for a husband. If marriage is what they wanted most they could have had it long ago. Hundreds of them had offers of marriage here in the homeland before they ever went to the field, but turned them down because they were convinced that the Lord wanted them in missionary work. Having once put their hand to the plow they refused to turn back.

And how does it work out when they sublimate their desire for marriage to the greater glory of God? For the most part it works out amazingly well. These single women are among the finest missionaries to be found anywhere. In spite of the handicaps under which they live, they do a remarkably good job. They are well-integrated personalities. They adjust readily to new circumstances and situations. They are cheerful, conscientious, hard-working, and cooperative. They have hardly any household duties to perform and no children to worry about; consequently they have more time to devote to the Lord's work. They are free to come and go as they wish. It is much easier for them than for married women to keep open house. In this way they get closer to the people, especially the women and children. Having more time to devote to language study, they usually become better speakers than the married women.

It is interesting to note in this connection that those missions that are working in the more primitive regions of the world, where both life and work are hard, usually have a higher than average ratio of women to men. In some missions they outnumber the men two and three to one. Pioneer work used to be reserved for single men; but now that they are a vanishing breed, much pioneer work has to be done by the single women. In fact, in many parts of the world they are doing the kind of work that should be required only of men. But they do it cheerfully as unto the Lord and ask no questions.

There are, of course, some disadvantages under which the single ladies must work. The first of these is a certain stigma that is associated with the single state in a culture where celibacy is unknown. The single person naturally sticks out like a sore thumb. Curiosity is aroused and embarrassing questions may be asked. However, this is not as troublesome as it might appear. When the questions have all been answered and rapport has been established, the single missionary fits into the landscape without much difficulty. Certainly in church circles her celibacy is understood. Then again, in the Buddhist countries of Southeast Asia and the Far East male and female celibacy is practiced in the *Sangha*—the monastic order. So in that part of the world religious celibates pose no problem.

In some parts of the world, especially where the Confucian ethic has spread, there is a clear line of demarcation between the sexes. Men fellowship with men, and women with women. In such a culture the single women missionaries find that much of their work is confined to the women and children. But this is no great drawback. The male missionaries can't very well minister to the womenfolk; so the single ladies concentrate on that segment of the population. So it works out quite well—the men missionaries ministering to the men and the women missionaries working with the women.

There is one other problem. In most parts of the Third World the Women's Liberation Movement is still unknown. Society is still dominated by the menfolk and the women are happy to have it that way. This means that when a church comes into being it too will be dominated by men. Naturally the leaders will have some difficulty in adjusting to the presence of women missionaries in the church. The latter will have to be as wise as serpents and as harmless as doves to work harmoniously with church leaders who are unaccustomed to dealing with women on a basis of equality.

When all is said and done, single women missionaries have a strategic role to play on the mission field, and with few exceptions they play it well. Young women looking forward to the mission field have nothing to fear. If they go at God's command, He will have a place for them to fill.

7. Fear of failure. So much has been said of the hardships of missionary life and the high qualifications for missionary service that many young Christians have been turned aside. They say to themselves: "If missionary life is that difficult, I might as well forget about it. I just don't have what it takes." The fear of failure is very real and acts as a strong deterrent. Through the years thousands of young people have been kept from going into missionary work because of a sense of inadequacy.

What about hardships? Are they really as great as we have been led to believe? Much depends on what part of the world one has in mind. The missionaries in Japan have all the amenities of modern life that we enjoy here in the United States. The climate is moderate; the food plentiful and nutritious. The trains are newer, cleaner, and faster than ours. The literacy rate is the highest in the world. The architecture and the gardens are exquisitely beautiful. The people are clever, courteous, industrious, and immaculately clean. Hardship? The two thousand missionaries in Japan don't know what it is.

There are, of course, other parts of the world where life is not quite so pleasant; but even there the picture has often been overdrawn. Most missionaries would have to acknowledge that upon arrival in the host country they found conditions better than they expected. Even in very primitive areas the missionaries manage to surround themselves with some of the *basic* comforts and conveniences of life.

More important is the fact that the human organism possesses an amazing capacity for survival. It does not die easily! Given time and patience the individual can adjust both physically and psychologically to almost any kind of environment. Upon arrival the appalling poverty that abounds on every hand seems to rise up and smite the new missionary in the face. The fact that the missionary with his meager resources cannot possibly alleviate the poverty only serves to aggravate the situation. But after a while he becomes inured to the strange sights and sounds and doesn't even notice them. That is nature's way of protecting the sensitive soul from the abrasive elements in the environment.

In addition to nature's healing ways there is the grace of God. Paul found it sufficient for him in his day, even with his thorn in the flesh (2 Co 12:9). Thousands of veteran missionaries can testify to the fact that Hudson Taylor, who spent fifty years in China, hit the nail on the head when he expressed his missionary creed in four clauses: "There is a living God. He has spoken in His Word. He means what He says. And He always keeps His promise."

The missionary does not go out alone, nor in his own strength. He is sent by the living Lord (Jn 20:21), who has promised to be with him to the end of the age (Mt 28:20). The Captain of his salvation is the same yesterday, today, and forever (Heb 13:8), and He has promised never to leave him nor forsake him (He 13:5). He will perfect that which concerns him (Ps 138:8). He will deliver him from every evil work and preserve him unto His heavenly kingdom (2 Ti 4:18).

If the misisonary is a missionary by the will of God, as Paul said he was, he need have no fear of failure. God will lead him in triumph (2 Co 2:14) and give him the victory (1 Co 15:57). It makes no difference whether it is a matter of learning a difficult language, or adjusting to a strange culture, or living with loneliness, the grace of God and the power of Christ can make the missionary more than conqueror (Ro 8:37) .

Obstacles to a Missionary Career

When the potential missionary has exploded all the myths and gotten rid of all the hang-ups, he is still not out of the woods. Even after he has dedicated his life to the Lord for missionary service there may still be obstacles in his way. As we sometimes say—there is many a slip 'twixt the cup and the lip. So there are many pitfalls between the decision to be a missionary and arrival on the field.

It has been estimated that for every hundred persons who dedicate their lives for missionary work only one actually gets to the field. It is impossible to say how accurate that figure is, for there is no possible way to check it; but it is safe to say that only a fraction of those who declare their willingness to go to the mission field ever get there.

There are many reasons for this. In the first place time is always a factor. Many persons register a decision in their teens before they realize what it is all about. Such a decision may not have been of the Lord to begin with. Others make the decision in good faith only to find it fade with the passing of time. Still others, for no particular reason, drift along with the crowd and eventually end up in secular work. And still others get into Christian work at home. The reasons are legion. We shall discuss only some of the more common obstacles.

1. **Advanced education.** Education is a splendid thing and every prospective missionary should get as much as he possibly can before going to the field. Most Americans contemplating missionary service will want to have at least a college degree. Up to this point they are fairly safe; but for every year they remain in this country after that their chances of getting to the field are correspondingly diminished. What is the reason for this?

It usually requires two full years to get an M.A. degree. During that time many things may happen to the prospective missionary. He may become so absorbed in his studies that he loses sight of the mission field and ends up in a teaching position here at home. If he goes off to seminary it will take him three years to graduate. During his seminary years he will be exposed more to the opportunities of the pastorate than to the claims of the mission field. He may decide that the Lord has called him to be a pastor, not a missionary.

And if he stays around long enough to get a Ph.D. his chances of getting to the mission field are drastically reduced. By this time he will have become a scholar, more interested in the pursuit of knowledge than in the propagation of the gospel. It *need* not be that way; it *should* not be that way; but in fact it often turns out that way. Most evangelists are not scholars; most scholars are not evangelists. The ideal missionary is one who has the mind of a scholar and the heart of an evangelist. Alas, that combination is very rare.

The person with advanced degrees may easily assume that the mission field does not offer sufficient scope for his many talents. To make the best use of his education he should remain at home where he can teach in a prestigious university.

This does not mean that any of these persons is necessarily out of the will of God. The Lord may have called them to teach in a university or to pastor a church. If so, there can be no quarrel with them. The fact remains—they are lost to the mission field.

2. **Accumulation of debts.** "Buy now and pay later" is the foundation stone of the American free enterprise system. With every passing year it becomes easier and easier to do just that. The only exception to this rule is the funeral service! And before long they may devise a way of taking care of that too.

The cost of higher education has risen so much in the last decade that tens of thousands of college students have been obliged to borrow money to put themselves through school. Uncle Sam doesn't charge any interest on his loans until after graduation; and if the borrower teaches public school his loan is reduced by 10 percent each year. With inflation as rampant as it is, it pays the student to borrow money rather than work for it.

This kind of arrangement is excellent for the average student. With a college degree under his belt he will be able to command a good salary and repay his loan in two or three years. But what about the prospective missionary who majors in Bible or missions? When he graduates he goes into Christian service where the salary scale is much lower than in business or the professions. If he has accumulated a sizable loan it may take him five or six years to liquidate it. By that time he may have settled down in the pastorate and decided to stay.

No reputable mission board will accept a candidate with a debt over his head. He must be free of all debts before he is permitted to proceed to the field. One candidate secretary has gone on record saying that he personally never knew of a single missionary candidate with a sizable debt who ever got to the mission field. It takes too long for Christian workers to liquidate their debts.

Prospective missionary doctors are particularly vulnerable at this point, and for two reasons. First, their academic career is so long that they are pushing thirty by the time they are ready to practice. Second, the cost of that kind of education may run as high as forty or fifty thousand dollars. Unless he has a rich uncle the medical student will have to borrow most of that money; and it will take him years before he is free of debt. By that time he will be pushing thirty-five, will have begun to raise a family, and will have established his own practice. To pull up stakes at that point and give up a lucrative profession to move to the mission field is a difficult decision to make. This is why medical missionaries today are in such short supply, and why mission after mission is crying out for them.

3. Love and marriage. Only the Lord knows exactly how many people have fallen by the way on this account. But the number must be very high. According to several recent studies a significant number of persons who opt for the mission field make their decision during their teens before they ever get to college. While in college they make many friends and in the process may fall in love. The other partner may be a good Christian but one who has no call to full-time Christian work and certainly no intentions of going to the mission field.

Occasionally the missionary-minded student will win the other partner to his or her point of view, and together they will prepare for missionary service. They may even get married before leaving for the field. But that is the exception, not the rule. Oftener than not the missionary-minded one gradually loses his missionary vision and is lost to the mission field.

There are, of course, some shining exceptions. The author personally knows of a number of persons whose dedication to the Lord and His service was strong enough to overcome every other consideration. Some of these went to the mission field at great sacrifice to themselves only to find that the Lord had someone waiting for them when they got there. Others have waited patiently for years until the Holy Spirit spoke to the reluctant partner and he or she eventually joined them on the mission field.

Others get married when they are quite young and by the time they are ready to go to the field they have two or three children. This may pose a problem, depending on the mission of one's choice. A generation ago this problem did not exist. At that time the vast majority of candidates were young and single. Today's youth are marrying at a younger age, many of them while still in college. Moreover, more of them are remaining at home for an extra year or two to pick up an advanced degree. Consequently it is not uncommon for candidates to have one or two children by the time they apply to the mission.

As might be expected, policy differs from mission to mission. There are not more than one or two boards that will accept a couple regardless of the number of children they have. Most boards draw the line at two; some reduce it to one. There are a few boards that refuse to accept a couple with even one child.

In this, as in most other things, the mission boards have good reasons for the policies they adopt. Experience has taught them that adjustment to a different culture and the learning of a foreign language are achieved with greater facility and success if the persons involved can give all their time and thought to the business at hand. Young mothers with children seldom achieve either accuracy or fluency in a foreign tongue; and this, of course, hampers their usefulness for the whole of their missionary career.

4. **Parental opposition.** This is a greater obstacle than most people think. There are two kinds of opposition. One kind comes from non-Christian parents who have no use for religion, much less missions. The other comes from Christian parents, some of them evangelical, who believe in missions but are unhappy when *their* children become involved.

In the case of non-Christian parents, sometimes the opposition assumes violent, almost paranoiac, proportions. The author is personally acquainted with fellows and girls who have been locked out of their own homes for no other offense than announcing their intention to become missionaries. Some have been completely disowned by their families. Others have had their names removed from their father's will.

One mother was so sick at the thought of her daughter's going to the mission field that when it came time for her to leave the mother went to bed, turned her face to the wall, and refused to say good-bye. For seven years the daughter wrote regularly to her mother; but she didn't get so much as a postcard in reply. It was not until she returned on furlough that the mother finally relented and was reconciled to her daughter. This is by no means an unusual case.

The opposition that comes from Christian parents is more silent and more subtle but none the less damaging. Such parents are in favor of Christian missions and give generously to the cause; but they are less than happy when their *own* son or daughter decides on a missionary career. That brings the matter a little too close to home. Missions is all right for the other fellow's son or daughter but not for theirs. They have grandiose plans for their children and these don't include the mission field. The father may want his son to succeed him in the business, which may have been in the family for several generations. The pressure generated by this kind of situation is sometimes harder to resist than the outright opposition of non-Christian parents.

What should young people do when they find themselves in that kind of predicament? Filial piety is a Christian virtue, and under ordinary circumstances children are obliged to obey their parents, especially when they are Christians. But nowhere does the Bible suggest that parents, Christian or non-Christian, have the right to come between their children and the will of God. From a purely human point of view it is wrong for parents to force their plans on their children. It is doubly wrong when those plans run contrary to the will of God.

If the parents are old, or ill, or poor, or for some other reason are absolutely dependent on their son or daughter for their livelihood, then the young person should give serious consideration to what Paul had to say to Timothy: "If any one does not provide for his relatives, and especially for his own family, he has disowned the faith and is worse than an unbeliever" (1 Ti 5:8). After much prayer and soul-searching he may decide that the Lord would have him remain at home, at least for the time being, to fulfill his Christian duty to his parents. Missionaries in mid-career have been known to remain at home for five or ten years to minister to the needs of aging parents. But 1 Timothy 5:8 should not be applied to well-meaning but self-centered parents who are unwilling to give their children to the Lord for His service.

In that case the young person should be guided by the words of Christ: "He who loves father or mother more than me is not worthy of me; and he who loves son or daughter more than me is not worthy of me" (Mt 10:37).

It should, however, be borne in mind that when we obey the teaching of Scripture the Lord has a way of working on our behalf and giving us the desire of our hearts (Ps 37:4). And in the case of those who have left family and loved ones He has given His word of promise: "Truly, I say to you, there is no one who has left house or brothers or sisters or mother or father or children or lands, for my sake and for the gospel, who will not receive a hundredfold now in this time . . . and in the age to come eternal life" (Mk 10:29-30).

God is no man's debtor. He has said, "Those who honor me I will honor" (1 Sa 2:30). If we obey Him, He will be responsible for all the consequences that flow from our obedience. Missionaries have given their children to the Lord only to find that He takes better care of them than they themselves could have done. There are missionaries who have given up parents only to find that He makes ample provision for them, far exceeding anything the missionaries could have asked or thought (Eph. 3:20).

On the other hand, parents have refused to allow their children to go to the mission field only to find that the children turned out to be a sorrow to them in their old age.

5. Health problems. Most mission boards maintain high health standards and anyone who falls below them is rejected. The health standards maintained by the Peace Corps are considerably lower than those demanded by the average mission board. The Peace Corps volunteer spends only twenty-one months overseas, whereas the missionary usually serves for life; and this makes a big difference.

Mission boards have been criticized for rejecting people on health grounds; but experience has taught them that a poor risk can turn out to be very costly, not only for the mission but also for the missionary. Missions are supported by the churches, and they feel an obligation to be faithful in the exercise of their stewardship.

The average missionary doesn't reach his full potential until his second term of service. To send a family to the field, and keep them there for four years, is a costly undertaking. It might run as high as $30,000. If for any reason the family doesn't return for a second term that huge investment is lost. Little wonder that the mission boards are reluctant to take the risk of accepting a person with a health problem.

Mission boards are not infallible, and so they make mistakes. One man from Scotland was turned down by the China Inland Mission but accepted by the British and Foreign Bible Society, with whom he served for thirty years in Singapore. On the other hand missions have been known to accept persons who seemed to be in good health only to discover that they cracked up within a year.

It is always disappointing for a young person to pass all the other tests and then to be rejected on health grounds. More than one young lady has dissolved into tears when the final verdict became known. It is equally disappointing for the mission. Good candidates are not so plentiful that mission boards can afford to turn them down. It is an agonizing decision to make.

The candidate who has offered for overseas service and has been rejected at least has the satisfaction of knowing that he followed the Lord to the end of the trail and gave up only when the way was closed. Such people usually find their way into some form of full-time Christian service at home. They never lose their interest in missions and quite frequently are instrumental in sending others to the field. So the venture is by no means lost. And the Lord will say to all such persons, as He said to David, "You did well that it was in your heart" (1 Kg 8:18).

6. Lack of direction. Modern youth is restive, uncertain, confused, and sometimes frightened. Human problems are so enormous that they defy solution. Personal options are so numerous that they cause confusion. And today's young people are caught between the problems and the options and hardly know how to relate the one to the other. In such a complex situation it is difficult to make up one's mind. It is not uncommon for students to reach their senior year and still not know what they are going to do. By the time June rolls round they are in the throes of "senior panic."

One problem is that today's students, with their knowledge of psychology, anthropology, and sociology, are tempted to lean on their own understanding (Pr 3:5) rather than look to the Lord for His direction and guidance. Some years ago a student of mine was approaching graduation and was still uncertain about his future. He was a good Christian fellow who, when he entered college, had definite plans to enter the ministry. Now he was not so sure. So I asked him, "Jim, do you ever pray about this matter? Have you ever asked the Lord to guide you with regard to your lifework?"

He replied, "Oh, I take God for granted. He is always in the back of my mind. I make my decisions as best I can in the light of what I know about myself, and I trust Him to keep me from going wrong."

Then again, there is the problem of understanding what Christian missions is all about. There are many fine Christian students today who have a passing interest in missions and from time to time have an urge to participate; but they don't have sufficient information to enable them to make an intelligent decision one way or the other. Their knowledge of missions is derived largely from missionary speakers in church or chapel whose messages tend to center around their own local work. Seldom do they hear a message that deals with the major issues of Christian missions on anything like a global scale. Consequently their knowledge of missions is fragmentary and superficial. What they know seems to intrigue them; but they don't know enough to enable them to make a definite commitment.

There is no substitute for knowledge. The best form of inspiration is information. Alas, it is possible for students to attend a Christian liberal arts college for four years and never be required to read a single book on church history or world missions. It is pertinent to ask: "In what sense is a college Christian if it does not include in its offerings those courses which might conceivably lead the graduates into full-time Christian service, either at home or overseas?" This is usually left to the inspiration provided by chapel services, prayer meetings, and spiritual emphasis week. These are good, to be sure, but hardly provide a solid foundation on which to build a missionary vocation.

7. Lack of Bible training. The conservative mission boards require their candidates to have a working knowledge of the Bible. The absolute minimum is one year of formal Bible training. Some Bible colleges have a special one-year program designed to meet this particular need. Several seminaries now have a one-year program in Biblical studies leading to a Master of Arts in Religion degree. The ideal preparation for missionary service is four years of liberal arts and three years of seminary with a concentration in missions. In this way the candidate gets a good foundation in all three major areas: liberal arts, theological studies, and missiology. Another very acceptable program is that offered by the four-year Bible colleges. Traditionally they have provided the lion's share of missionary candidates for the conservative missions.

Even specialists, such as doctors and nurses, are required to have *some* Bible training. The rationale for this requirement is that the candidate is first a missionary and only secondarily a doctor or a nurse or some other specialist. Consequently he is expected to have a good grasp of the major doctrines of the Christian faith and be able to explain them to others. The year of extra study will also provide an opportunity to pick up some courses in personal evangelism, non-Christian religions, and cross-cultural communications, all designed to help him articulate his faith when he gets to the mission field. Without this additional training he may be a competent doctor, but he will be a poor communicator. To be a *missionary* doctor he ought to be good at both.

The problem arises when a graduate of the secular university offers for missionary service. His academic record may be impeccable, but because he lacks Bible and theology he is disqualified. Even a person from a Christian liberal arts college will run into trouble at this point. Unless he has majored in Bible he will have only two or three Bible survey courses to his credit, and that is not enough. So the mission board says to the candidate: "Fine, you have a good, sound liberal arts education; now you must go back to school to get at least one year of concentrated Bible and theology."

With some people this is no great problem. They understand the reason for the requirement and are quite willing to cooperate. They are still young and consequently not averse to returning to school for another year. With others it may be a problem, depending on age, finances, and family circumstances, etc. Some people have been in school so long that the thought of another year of the academic rat race is not a pleasant prospect. Others simply balk at the requirement and withdraw their offer for missionary service.

8. Lack of practical experience. There is a growing recognition on the part of educators of the importance of in-service training. The American Association of Theological Schools is now insisting that all its member schools strengthen their field education programs. The minimum requirement is nine hours of field education under proper supervision. To put teeth into the program academic credit is given.

One of the outstanding features of the Bible college movement has been the insistence on Christian service. Every student is required to engage in some form of Christian service during his entire course of study. Up to this point it has not carried academic credit; but it has been required right across the board. The theories learned in the classroom are tested in the laboratory of experience. In this way the student gains valuable experience while he is learning. In fact, learning by doing is now an accepted principle of modern pedagogy. The student with three or four years of experience in Christian service makes a better missionary candidate.

Most Christian liberal arts colleges have a Christian service department. While Christian service is not required, it is definitely encouraged. It is estimated that about 50 percent of the students engage in some form of Christian service during the course of the academic year.

It goes without saying that the secular universities have no such program. Christian students in these institutions can, if they wish, find their own Christian service; but not many go to the trouble.

The missionary candidate who has had little or no practical experience will encounter grave difficulty when he meets the mission board. Even if he is qualified in all other respects he will not be accepted without sufficient practical experience. What usually happens is that the board will accept him *tentatively* on condition that he spend eight or nine months at Missionary Internship in Detroit. There he will be placed in a church where he will work closely with the pastor and engage in the various kinds of ministry usually connected with the local church. During this time he will be under the supervision of Missionary Internship personnel. When the period is over MI will evaluate his work and send a report to the mission. If the report is favorable his tentative acceptance will be changed to total acceptance; if not, he will be turned down. It is important that young people looking forward to missionary service should get as much practical training as possible during their college career.

So important is Christian service training that some mission boards now require all candidates, regardless of their background or experience, to spend two years in the pastorate before going overseas. This is particularly true of all missionaries looking forward to church-planting work.

9. Attractive offers at home. This is the final hurdle and many a young man has failed to clear it successfully.

It is an excellent idea to get two years of experience in some form of ministry in the homeland before proceeding to the field; *but* during that time many things can happen. Some candidates get married to a person who does not share their missionary vision. Others become so absorbed in the work they are doing that they lose contact with the mission and by and by lose their missionary burden. Still others are so successful that the churches are reluctant to release them when the two years are up. Not all churches are as magnanimous as the one in Antioch, which was willing to part with its best teachers,

Barnabas and Saul, when the Holy Spirit called them into missionary service (Acts 13:1-3).

Not a few missionary candidates have ended up in the pastorate here because of the pressure brought to bear on them by well-meaning but short-sighted churches. The author knows of one large church that offered its youth director a substantial increase in salary if he would give up the idea of going to Africa. Fortunately he had the fortitude to stick to his guns and do what he believed the Lord wanted him to do.

The longer the missionary candidate remains in Christian work at home and the more successful he is, the greater is the temptation to remain in this country.

Qualifications for Missionary Service

In the nineteenth century the missionary was regarded as a hero. It was assumed that he was an intellectual and spiritual giant, more dedicated, more courageous, and more spiritual than his counterpart, the pastor here at home. Today the pendulum has swung in the opposite direction, and today's missionary is in danger of being reduced to the status of a "humdrum worker in the vineyard of the Lord." Students returning from a summer of missionary work overseas report that their greatest discovery was that missionaries are human after all. In our reaction against the adulation of the past we may be in danger of underestimating the qualities of today's missionary.

Stephen Neill, himself a missionary of no mean stature, wrote:

> I may place on record my conviction that the needs of the mission field are always far greater than the needs of the Church at home, that no human qualifications, however high, render a man or woman more than adequate for missionary work, that there is no career which affords such scope for enterprise and creative work, and that in comparison with the slight sacrifice demanded, the reward is great beyond all measuring.[1]

Most mission societies screen their candidates very carefully. This they do for two reasons. First, they want to reduce as far as possible the number of dropouts. Second, they want to be sure that they get the highest possible caliber of missionary. The best is none too good for the mission field.

There are almost five hundred missionary agencies based in North America. Naturally they don't all have the same standards. Some accept only seminary graduates. Others will accept college graduates.

---

[1] Stephen Neill, *Builders of the Indian Church* (London: Edinburgh House Press, 1934), p. 4.

Still others, with lower standards, accept Bible school graduates. Some insist on very high academic qualifications but don't worry too much about spiritual qualifications. Others are very particular about spiritual qualifications but don't hassle over academic qualifications. There are others that do their best to maintain high standards in both areas.

The perfect missionary has not yet appeared on the scene; and it would be foolish and futile to insist on standards bordering on perfection. On the other hand it would be a grave mistake to suggest that any Tom, Dick, or Harry, without any special training or any particular qualifications, can make an acceptable missionary. He need not be a genius; but he had better not be a dunce either.

The qualifications of a good missionary break down into several categories.

1. **Physical qualifications.** High schools, colleges, the Peace Corps, and the United States Army all require a physical examination before accepting the applicant. The reasons for this are obvious. Mission boards have additional reasons to be careful about the health of their applicants. Life on the mission field, with few exceptions, is harder on one's health than life here at home. Contributing factors include hot, humid climate, poor food, contagious diseases, and lack of public sanitation. Medical facilities are either nonexistent or in short supply. Some families live in isolated areas where the nearest doctor or hospital may be a three-day journey away. When casualties occur they are very costly to both the missionary and the mission.

For this reason all missions require a complete medical checkup. They are particularly wary of any signs of high blood pressure, impaired sight or hearing, nervous disorders, allergies, etc. Physical deformities such as blindness, deafness, artificial limbs, etc., are almost sure to disqualify the applicant. Some physical defects can be removed by surgery, after which the applicant will be accepted. The candidate doesn't have to be a physical giant or have a near-perfect physique; but he must have a good, consistent, all-round health record. Any chronic ailment, however slight, is apt to be aggravated on the mission field. It is always a tragedy when an otherwise fully qualified candidate is rejected for health reasons.

2. **Academic qualifications.** For the most part the mainline denominations have maintained fairly high academic standards. Even in the nineteenth century most of their missionaries were college or seminary graduates. When Hudson Taylor came along and started the faith missions movement he appealed for those "of little formal education." When the Bible schools got under way on this continent in the last decades of the nineteenth century they too accepted those

of little formal education, and gave them enough Bible training to enable them to become effective lay workers in the Christian church. It comes as no surprise to learn that most of the Bible school graduates who went overseas joined the faith missions. In recent decades both the Bible schools and the faith missions have raised their academic standards. Most of the larger schools are now degree-granting institutions.

Most missions prefer their candidates to have at least a college education. Beyond that the higher they go the better. The demands on today's missionary are so great that he should get as much education as he possibly can before going to the field. Only so will he be able to cope with the intellectual, social, political, and religious problems he is likely to encounter in the course of his missionary career. This is especially true if he plans to work among students and other intellectuals.

At the same time it should be recognized that a college or seminary education is no guarantee of genuine intellectual prowess—at least not here in the United States, where higher education is accessible to all. On the mission field there are hundreds of older missionaries who never had a chance to go to college, but they have something that no college can impart, intellectual capacity. They are largely self-educated but can hold their own with the best of them. The real test of a person's intellectual prowess is whether he keeps on growing after his formal education has ceased.

3. Vocational qualifications. We hear a great deal today about specialization, not only at home but also on the mission field. Most missionaries need some technical or vocational training over and above their liberal arts education. All missionaries, regardless of their area of specialization, should have a thorough understanding of missiology, including the history, theology, philosophy, and methodology of missions, non-Christian religions, cross-cultural communications, missionary anthropology, area studies, church planting, etc. Those going into Bible translation work should have a mastery of Greek and Hebrew and be completely conversant with the language and culture of the host country. This has not always been the case.

> Out of some 1,500 evangelical missionaries in Japan recently not one could be found who was competent enough in both languages to check a new Japanese translation against the original Hebrew. Liberals and Roman Catholics could have done it—but not the evangelicals.[2]

---

[2] Michael Griffiths, *Give Up Your Small Ambitions* (London: Inter-Varsity Press, 1970), p. 50.

Much depends, of course, on the kind of work into which the specialist goes. The larger missions have room for all kinds of specialists in the areas of theology, teaching, medicine, evangelism, radio and television, literature, journalism, youth work, business, finance, accounting, secretarial work, linguistics, aviation, etc. There is a crying need for specialists in all these areas. The tragedy is that in many instances these roles are now being filled by persons without any special or technical training for the tasks they are performing. They mean well; they work long and hard; and they are doing a tolerably good job; but they lack professional competence and the work suffers accordingly. The time is long past when we can do a second-rate job and expect to get away with it.

Topflight theologians are desperately needed on the mission field. Until such time as they are forthcoming it will be necessary for church leaders from the Third World to come to the West for their theological training. It would be much better, and certainly much cheaper, to educate them in their own countries.

4. Psychological qualifications. By psychological qualifications we really mean personality traits. Personality traits are more important in some roles than in others.

> A bookkeeper doesn't have to worry about the impression he makes on anybody but the boss. The main thing is to have his records neat and accurate. That's not true of the salesperson, however. The volume of his sales and the commission he gets may depend on such impressions. A research scientist may be a very disagreeable person to meet, at the same time that he is highly regarded for his contribution to science. But a minister of the Gospel can't even get a hearing for his message if he continually rubs people the wrong way.[3]

Rubbing people the wrong way is a greater danger on the mission field than here at home, for the simple reason that missionaries have to live at close quarters. Some of them live on "stations" or "compounds" where they are thrown together with other missionaries twelve hours a day, seven days a week. If one person in the group is abrasive, he can make life miserable for the others. Nowhere are interpersonal relations more important than on the mission field. For this reason many missions are now administering psychological as well as medical tests to all candidates.

No matter how hard we try we will not be able to achieve the perfectly integrated personality; but human relations are greatly facilitated if the persons involved possess certain desirable personality traits.

---

[3] Harold C. Cook, *An Introduction to the Study of Christian Missions* (Chicago: Moody Press, 1954), p. 112.

a. Emotional stability. The wear and tear of life on the mission field is considerably greater than here at home. The difficulty lies not in the big crack-ups that come once or twice a decade but in the hundred-and-one little irritations that are part of everyday life. Over the long haul these can completely upset one's emotional equilibrium. Persons who are given to introspection, or have an inferiority complex, or are afflicted with phobias and frustrations of various kinds usually have a difficult time adjusting to the kind of communal life found in some parts of the mission field. Mental health and emotional immaturity account for 10.9 percent of all the dropouts on the mission field.

b. Adaptability. Confucius said on one occasion, "When you enter a new territory, be sure to inquire concerning its customs." The Western counterpart of that is, "When in Rome do as the Romans do." When the missionary from the West arrives in the East he finds himself in an entirely different world. Everything is different—climate, food, dress, language, religion, and customs. In a word, the entire culture is different from anything he has known up to that point.

Obviously if he is going to be a success he must adapt to the mores of the host country. This is absolutely necessary if he wants to make friends and influence people. Otherwise he will be just another "ugly American." The person who is unable to change his ways will probably not last more than a year or two on the mission field.

c. Sense of humor. Missionary work is serious business. It is the King's business and requires haste; but the missionary himself must not be *too* serious. He must not take his fellow missionaries too seriously. Above all he ought to be able to laugh at himself. Many a tense and potentially explosive situation can be avoided if he sees the humorous side of the picture.

Particularly irksome to some missionaries is the universal practice in the East of "talking price." On one occasion I was at the mercy of a group of rickshaw coolies in Nanking. I was escorting eight children with all their baggage back to school after the Christmas break. We needed nine rickshaws to take us from the ferry to the railway station, a distance of about three miles. To make matters worse it was raining. Knowing my predicament they began by asking an exorbitant price. We haggled back and forth for several minutes but they refused to come down to a reasonable figure. Finally I said to the leader, "Venerable Brother, you misunderstand me. I don't want to *buy* the rickshaws; I just want to *hire* them!" That brought the house down. The other coolies burst into laughter, and the leader said, "Okay. Okay. Let's go." And away we went to the railway station.

d. Spirit of cooperation. The missionary is a member of a team.

On the team are missionaries and nationals; he must learn to work harmoniously with both. He cannot be a lone eagle. There are too many jobs to be done, too many roles to be filled. He must be willing to step into the breach and do a job for which he may not be particularly well qualified. He cannot refuse to teach Old Testament in the Bible school because he did his graduate work in New Testament. He may even be asked to teach homiletics, not because the mission wants to punish him, but because it must be taught and there is no one else to do it.

It is at this point that members of the younger generation who insist on doing their own thing get into trouble. All of us need to give heed to the admonition of Paul: "Let each of you look not only to his own interests, but also to the interests of others" (Ph 2:4).

e. Willingness to take orders. Much of the paternalism has gone out of the missionary movement, and that is a good thing; but so long as there is a structured organization with a chain of command, somebody has to give the orders and others must accept them. Major decisions and policies must be made at the top and carried out by those lower down. This does not preclude the desirability of input at all levels; but the final decision must be made by the leaders, after which the rank and file are expected to fall into line.

In all well-ordered missions every effort is made to canvass the opinions of the membership; and annual conferences are held on the various fields when the missionaries have ample opportunity to air their grievances and present their points of view; but the responsibility for policy making rests with the leadership on the field. Above the field council is the home council or, in some missions, the international council, which is responsible for the total operation of the entire mission at home and overseas. The field council members must be willing to implement the policies laid down by the international council; and the missionaries must be prepared to abide by the decisions of the field council. There is no other way to operate an international organization.

f. Ability to endure hardness. The Chinese call it "eating bitterness." There is no doubt that the affluent society in which we live has produced in all of us a love of ease and comfort that is the hallmark of the American way of life. We have central heating in the winter and air conditioning in the summer and twenty-eight varieties of ice cream the year round. Physical well-being, financial security, material prosperity, peace and contentment, law and order—these are the main ingredients that go to make up the affluent society that is America. The individual is pampered and protected from the cradle to the grave. Dentistry, surgery, and now childbirth, are all rendered painless. Even Band-Aids must be "ouchless." The energy crisis that now threatens to change drastically the American life-style is perhaps the best thing that has happened to us since Thomas Edison invented the incandescent lamp.

The American missionary, more than any other, finds it difficult to knuckle down to the simple life-style in most parts of the Third World. Like the Children of Israel who hankered after the "leeks and onions of Egypt," he wants to retain as much as possible of the American standard of living. That is why some of them take tons of household stuff, including canned goods, when they leave for the field. In this respect the Peace Corps volunteers put the missionaries to shame. They live at the level of the people they serve. They are not allowed to own jeeps, cars, or even bicycles. They use public transportation, second class where available.

Most missionaries are married and have families, so they cannot be expected to compete with the Peace Corps; but they must be prepared to endure hardness, like good soldiers of Jesus Christ, in order to identify with the people they are seeking to win. The gap between the "have" nations and the "have not" nations is altogether too great. The Christian missionary by himself cannot close that gap no matter what he does, but he can help to bridge it at the local level if he is willing to "eat bitterness."

g. *Patience and perseverance.* The missionary is not going to change the world overnight. The East is agonizingly slow. The West is ridiculously fast. A man's whole day can be spoiled if the elevator in the office building takes him one floor beyond where he wants to go.

One of the most difficult adjustments for the missionary is to s-l-o-w d-o-w-n. In thirty-six hours he goes from the jet age to the ox age, and the sudden change can be traumatic. In all aspects of his life and work he will have need of patience and perseverance. Without these virtues he is almost sure to crack up. He may try to circumvent the problem by operating his own jeep; but he will still need patience when the jeep bogs down in two feet of mire or he comes to a river that has no bridge and the ferry is not operating. If he decides to go by bus he may find that the bus driver has decided to take the day off.

Government officials, church leaders, and the people in general are in no great rush to get things done. The missionary may have to wait nine months to get his car through Customs and another two years to get his driver's license. Church leaders also take their time in making decisions, and having made them are often slow in executing them. They see no need for haste and can't understand why the missionary should be upset by the delay. What isn't accomplished today can always be undertaken tomorrow—or the next day, or the next day after that. In the meantime they may discover that the decision wasn't a wise one to begin with and therefore need not be implemented at all. And all the while the American missionary is fussing and fuming, and sometimes fulminating.

h. *Without a superiority complex.* In the words of Kenneth Scott Latourette, the nineteenth-century missionary was "serenely convinced of the superiority of Western culture." In the missionary literature of that period the words "Christianity" and "civilization" were used almost interchangeably. The missionaries conceived of themselves as playing a civilizing as well as a Christianizing role. That day is gone. No missionary today would entertain such naive notions. Hopefully we know better.

That does not mean that we have licked the problem. It is still with us, albeit in more subtle forms. There are a hundred-and-one little ways in which the missionary may unconsciously reveal his superiority complex. There is an almost irresistible temptation to compare local products with their counterparts in the United States. Quite frequently they appear to be inferior in quality and craftsmanship. They don't work as well. They don't last as long. The missionary tosses them aside with some remark about "the crazy gadgets that don't work." His remarks may be heard only by his household servants; but that is enough. The word soon spreads throughout the community that the missionary doesn't like native products.

Indeed, the very fact that he arrives from the United States with nineteen drums of personal effects conveys the impression that American goods are superior to all others, else why would he go to all that trouble and expense?

The peoples of the Third World are doing their best to catch up with the technology of the West and are very self-conscious about the gap that still exists. Understandably they are touchy on these points and appreciate the missionary who has a genuine appreciation of them and their culture.

In most parts of the world the missionary is still treated with a certain degree of deference, partly as a carry-over from the past and partly because the Third World culture has always shown kindness and hospitality to strangers. It is very easy for the missionary to come to *expect* this kind of treatment and take offense if it is not forthcoming.

The missionary with his advanced degrees and his expertise may easily get a swelled head and think that he has all the answers and that the national leaders should listen to him and follow his advice. An attitude of superiority is something the missionary must guard against all the days of his life. It was bad enough in the nineteenth century; it is quite insufferable now.

i. *Without racial prejudice.* The white race has no monopoly on racial prejudice. The ancient Greeks divided the world into Greeks and barbarians. The Chinese called their country the "Middle Kingdom" and referred to all foreigners as barbarians. There is hardly a country in the world that does not have some form of racial prejudice.

On one occasion when riding the subway in New York City I saw an ad which contained only one word printed in large black letters on a white background—ECIDUJERP. For several minutes I could not figure out what it was all about. Then at the bottom of the ad, in small letters barely discernible, I read: "This word is PREJUDICE spelled backwards. Whichever way you spell it, it doesn't make sense." But sense or nonsense, it still persists in almost every society.

The problems relating to racism in the United States have been published in all the major newspapers of the world. There are people in the Third World who have never heard of Chicago or San Francisco who are well acquainted with Little Rock and Birmingham. Martin Luther King is almost as well known as John F. Kennedy.

It wouldn't be so bad if racism were confined to American society, but it has infected the churches as well. Indeed, the eleven o'clock hour on Sunday morning is the most segregated hour of the week. This sad fact has not gone unnoticed by foreign nationals in this country. Racism in America is a millstone around the neck of the missionary, especially in Africa.

In its more blatant forms racism has disappeared from the mission field; but there are a hundred-and-one subtle ways in which it can still be seen. It comes out not so much in the conduct of his work as in various aspects of his social life. It is one thing to *work* with the nationals on a basis of equality; it is another to *play* with them on the same basis. There is still a tendency for missionaries to seek the company of fellow missionaries or other Americans residing in a large city. The real test of a missionary's love for the people will be shown in the friends with whom he shares his leisure time.

Racial prejudice is particularly unfortunate in the Christian missionary—for two reasons. First, it is a denial of the teachings of Christ. Second, it alienates the very people he is trying to win.

5. Spiritual qualifications. If the missionary is not in every sense of the word a "man of God" he might as well remain at home. "It cannot be too positively asserted that missionary work is a spiritual enterprise, undertaken for spiritual results to be achieved only by spiritual means. It follows, therefore, that the essential qualifications are spiritual."[4]

a. Genuine conversion experience. It is hardly necessary to belabor this point. To be a missionary a person must have an evangelical fervor

---

[4] Rowland Hogben, *In Training* (Chicago: Inter-Varsity Christian Fellowship, 1946), p. 30.

growing out of a conversion experience. This is very important in a so-called Christian society where everyone whose name appears on a church roll is assumed to be a Christian. Some of the most zealous missionaries are those from a "pagan" background who were soundly converted to Christ after they reached college. Inter-Varsity Christian Fellowship and Campus Crusade for Christ play a major role at this point. The missionary who is not sure of his own salvation is not likely to lead others to a saving knowledge of Christ.

b. Knowledge of the Scriptures. The missionary's chief task is to share Jesus Christ with the non-Christian world. All he knows about Christ he learned from the Bible. Therefore it behooves him to have a thorough working knowledge of the Scriptures, which are able to make men wise unto salvation (2 Ti 3:15). No amount of worldly wisdom can substitute for a knowledge of the Scriptures. The missionary not only should know their contents but also have a thorough understanding of the major doctrines concerning God, man, sin, salvation, etc.

Moreover, the Scriptures are the source from which he gets the sustenance necessary for his spiritual life. They provide him with his message and his mandate. They are his chart and compass. They are his trustworthy guide in all matters pertaining to faith and morals. From them he derives wisdom, counsel, comfort, encouragement, and cleansing. In short, the Bible is the foundation on which he builds both his life and his work. Without a thorough knowledge of it the missionary is at a serious disadvantage.

c. Assurance of divine guidance. Missionary work is not getting any easier. Some of the physical hardships have been eliminated, but in their place is a whole host of other difficulties, psychological, ideological, and interpersonal. The short-termer may be able to get along fairly well without any great "sense of call," but the career missionary will find it mighty handy when the going gets rough. It will help him immensely if he can say, "I am a missionary by the will of God."

Two journalists, both agnostics, spent three months with missionaries in East Africa to see what makes them tick. In their report they made the following observation. "It is obvious when you talk to missionaries, and still more obvious on reflection, that the phenomenon of missionary work really makes sense only if their belief in a calling is taken at its face value.... Virtually everyone we met really did feel that in some deep sense they had surrendered their own will for that of another way of life—for their Lord, as they would put it."[5]

If a missionary has a deep, abiding conviction that he is in Brazil, or Borneo, or Burundi by the will of God he will not turn and run

[5] Helen and Richard Exley, *In Search of the Missionary* (London: Highway Press, 1970), p. 38.

at the first sight or sound of danger, nor will he give up when the difficulties multiply and the frustrations almost drive him crazy. He will go the second mile and stay on the job long after the sun has gone down only if he is sure that he is in the will of the Lord.

d. Strong devotional life. The devotional life of the missionary is all-important. He neglects it at his peril. He will be a man of God only if his spiritual life is systematically developed by daily Bible study, prayer, meditation, and worship.

Here at home, especially in seminary or Bible college, the student is buoyed up and carried along by the spiritual support provided by the Christian community of which he is a part: prayer meetings, chapel services, dorm fellowships, rap sessions, etc. On the mission field these props are largely missing. The missionary is on his own. He can't depend on others for fellowship or growth. He must know how to cultivate his own spiritual life without any outside help. Like the date tree whose taproot enables it to flourish even in the desert, he must have roots that go down deep. Otherwise his spiritual life will wither and die.

Hudson Taylor was one of the missionary giants of the nineteenth century whose name is a household word in evangelical circles. It was said of him that never once in fifty years did the sun rise in China without finding Hudson Taylor on his knees.

Most missionaries would have to confess that this is one of their greatest problems. They are constantly ministering to others; nobody ministers to them. If they don't set aside and jealously guard the "quiet time" each morning they will soon find themselves robbed of their joy as well as their power.

e. Self-discipline. Discipline seems to be essential to the ongoing of human society. Without it community life tends to disintegrate. There are two kinds of discipline. One is imposed from without; the other is cultivated from within. Most people have to rely on the first because they possess so little of the second. This is why we hear so much talk about "law and order." Apparently it is impossible to achieve the one without the other.

The missionary, more than anyone else, is dependent on *self-discipline.* Even the pastor at home is not in the same class with the missionary. The pastor is constantly under the surveillance of the people who pay his salary. If he falls down on the job he will be called before the church board to give an account of himself. More than one pastor has been asked to terminate his service for that reason. What about the missionary? Who is to check up on him? He may not see the field director more than once a year. If he loafs on the job or becomes lazy in body or mind he can easily get away with it.

Self-discipline is listed by Paul as one of the fruits of the Spirit in Galatians 5:23, where it is called "self-control." Even the great apostle had problems along this line. He said, "Every athlete exercises self-control in all things. They do it to receive a perishable wreath; but we an imperishable. Well, I do not run aimlessly, I do not box as one beating the air; but I pommel my body and subdue it, lest after preaching to others I myself should be disqualified" (1 Co 9:25-27).

f. *A heart of love.* Love is the hallmark of the Christian life (Jn 13:34-35) and the *sine qua non* of Christian service (1 Co 13:1-3). Jesus Christ, as the first and chief Missionary, came into the world to express the Father's love (Jn 3:16). The missionary goes into the world to express Christ's love. Paul and the other apostles were so controlled by the love of Christ (2 Co 5:14) that they were willing to risk their lives for the sake of the Lord Jesus Christ (Acts 15:26).

Writing to the little mission church in Thessalonica, Paul could say, "So being affectionately desirous of you, we were ready to share with you not only the gospel of God but also our own selves, because you had become very dear to us" (1 Th 2:8). Missionaries don't have to be bright or brave to be successful (though both are very desirable qualities), but they *must* be loving. The nationals will overlook many weaknesses and forgive many blunders if they are persuaded that the missionary has a heart of love.

g. *Some success in Christian service.* Important as the above-mentioned qualifications are, they are not sufficient. In addition there should be some evidence of fruitfulness in Christian service here at home. Before setting out for distant shores he should have proved himself in church or mission work at home. If he can't win souls in his own culture, what reason is there to believe he will do better in a foreign culture? Is he going to be an evangelistic missionary? Then there should be some evidence that he has the gift of evangelism. Does he hope to be a Bible teacher? Then he should have demonstrated that he possesses the gift of teaching.

There should be some evidence of God's blessing in his life and some proof of the power of the Holy Spirit in his ministry before he ventures overseas. Of one thing he can be sure: Success will not come more easily on the mission field.

3

The Magnitude of the Task

Predicting the future is always a risky thing to do. We are living in a rapidly changing world and anything could happen in the next five or ten years, including the return of Christ. Moreover, the Christian mission has traditionally operated in the Third World, where political stability is an unknown quantity. Even here in the United States we can't be sure what the future holds for us. Our own political institutions are being shaken to their foundations and the highest offices in the land are honeycombed with corruption. Every passing day brings additional ugly facts to light and we wonder where it is all going to end.

Developing Trends

Of one thing we can be sure: The Christian mission will continue to the end of the age in spite of the many changes that will take place. When Jesus Christ gave the Great Commission to His apostles He indicated quite clearly that the mandate was to extend to the end of the age (Mt 28:20). The Christian mission was not to terminate with the apostolic era, or the Middle Ages, or the Reformation period; it was to continue to the end of the age.

During the intervening period there would be wars and rumors of wars and all kinds of opposition and persecution. The disciples would be hated of all men. The missionary enterprise would be involved in all kinds of difficulties and dangers. The messengers of the cross would be hunted and hounded from pillar to post. They would be scourged in the Jewish synagogues and beaten by Roman officials. Indeed, some of them would lay down their lives for the sake of the gospel. But the mandate would never be rescinded nor the mission aborted. If the disciples were persecuted in one city they were not to call it quits, but move on to the next city.

Neither the mischief of men nor the machinations of the devil were to deter them. They were taught to believe that they were engaged in a Holy War with an implacable foe who would not surrender without a life-and-death struggle. Casualties would occur and reverses come, but they were to press on in the full assurance that the Captain of their salvation would be with them to the end of the age. Many battles would be lost, but the war would be won. On that point there was no doubt.

We do well to bear this in mind when the prophets of doom are sounding the death knell of the Christian mission. The days are dark and doors are closing in various parts of the world. Some timid souls are afraid that we are about to witness the demise of the missionary enterprise; but such is not the case. Dictators come and go; kingdoms rise and fall; civilizations wax and wane; but the worldwide mission of the Church will continue to the end of the age in spite of all the vicissitudes of human history. When one door closes another will open. If Western missionaries become *personae non gratae*, non-Western missionaries will be raised up to take their place. If *all* expatriate missionaries are expelled from a given country, the indigenous church will remain to carry on. If the indigenous church is forced to go underground, the Spirit of God, who dwells not in temples made with hands but in the hearts of His people, will be there. It is one thing to get rid of the visible Church; it is quite another to get rid of Almighty God. Heaven is His throne and earth is His footstool. It is impossible to banish Him from any part of His domain.

Problems will doubtless increase, difficulties will abound, costs will soar, but the mission will go on. God, who is able to make the wrath of man to praise Him (Ps 76:10) will see to that.

There is reason to believe that the rapid decline in missionary interest and activity on the part of the main-line denominations will continue in the days to come. A recent study showed that the total number of missionaries in six large denominations dropped from 3,160 in 1971 to 1,985 in 1979. Their leaders give no indication that steps are being taken to reverse the downward trend. So we can expect the missions affiliated with the Division of Overseas Ministries of the National Council of Churches in the U.S.A. to assume less and less responsibility for the evangelization of the world. This means that the conservative missions will have to bear increasing responsibility for the worldwide mission of the Christian Church. This raises an important question: Can these missions get enough candidates year by year to expand their overseas operations? Between 1967 and 1977 the forty-five faith missions in the Interdenominational Foreign Mission Association reported an overall increase of 9.6 percent for the ten-year period, which is slightly less than 1 percent per year. This is not very encouraging in light of the fact that in recent years many of the candidates have been short-termers, not career missionaries. It should also be borne in mind that five additional missions joined the association during that period, and two have recently withdrawn.

Not all these faith missions are growing at the same rate. Some are barely holding their own. Most of them have registered modest gains. Two or three have actually fallen behind. Half a dozen have experienced large gains, in some cases well over 100 percent. The largest growth has occurred in the younger missions. The older and larger missions are finding it increasingly difficult to hold their own against the attrition occasioned by death and retirement. When they reach the 800- or 900-member mark they have a tendency to level off at that one point. Only two IFMA missions are now above the 1,000 mark—the Sudan Interior Mission and the Evangelical Alliance Mission, both of which are international in membership.

What is true of the IFMA is also true in the EFMA—the Evangelical Foreign Missions Association. Its member missions have registered modest growth in the past ten years and hopefully will be able to maintain the momentum. Though most of these missions are denominational, they face the same problems as the faith missions.

There are, of course, many missions that do not belong to either of these organizations. Their rate of growth has been higher than that of the IFMA or the EFMA. Some of these missions have experienced rapid growth in the past decade. Outstanding among them are Wycliffe Bible Translators, Southern Baptist Convention, and New Tribes Mission. It remains to be seen if they can maintain comparable growth during the coming decade.

One aspect of the present situation that augers well for the future of the missionary movement is the obvious working of the Holy Spirit in recent years. There is no doubt that the Jesus movement, the charismatic movement, and similar movements are bringing renewal to the churches throughout the world, especially here in the United States. Prayer cells and Bible study groups are springing up all over the country, many of them outside the organized churches. Tens of thousands of students and young people, inside and outside the churches, have been "turned on" to Jesus Christ. Thousands of these in the glow of their first love will find their way into Christian training institutions of one kind or another, and hopefully hundreds, maybe thousands, of them will turn up on the mission field. In the history of the church revival and missions have always gone hand in hand. There is no reason to believe it will be different this time. Already this renewal is reflected in seminary enrollment, which is on the increase, especially in the more conservative seminaries. Even in the liberal seminaries the prospective students are now inquiring about the spiritual climate of the school and showing an interest in prayer groups, Bible study, and the parish ministry, in contrast to a few years ago when social action was the craze.

One interesting facet of the situation is the increased number of seminary students now coming from the secular colleges and universities, and a corresponding decrease in those coming from the Christian and Bible colleges.

Many of these students were virtual pagans when first confronted with the claims of Christ by Inter-Varsity Christian Fellowship, Campus Crusade for Christ, the Navigators, and other evangelical agencies engaged in student work. Their conversion experience is usually a clear-cut one which leaves them with a sense of appreciation and dedication often lacking in Christians who have come up through evangelical homes, churches, and colleges, and to whom the gospel is "old hat." These new converts have none of the hang-ups that plague students from a fundamentalist background. The Christian life to them is new and beautiful, and they have a deep desire to share it with others. Consequently they make good seminary students, and later on will make excellent missionaries.

There is likely to be a significant increase in the number of short-term missionaries in the years ahead. At present there are 8,600 short-termers out of a total of some 44,500 North American missionaries in all parts of the world. The program is obviously popular and is likely to attract an increasing number of youth in the coming decade. This will be prompted largely by two considerations: (1) The demand for career missionaries will certainly outstrip the supply and the gap will have to be filled by short-termers. (2) The thinking of today's youth is away from lifetime commitment in any area of endeavor. They want to look before they leap. They want to keep all options open. Recognizing this fact, some of the main-line denominations and at least one faith mission have already given up the idea of appealing for career missionaries, at least in the beginning.

During the coming decade the number of nonprofessional missionaries is likely to increase. Two factors will operate here: (1) With the rise of nationalism the professional missionary may become *persona non grata* in some parts of the world. If these countries are to continue to have a Christian witness it will be necessary for nonprofessional missionaries to take up the torch. This in turn will mean additional training. These nonprofessional missionaries, to be effective in their witness, should spend at least a year in a Bible college or seminary. With this new type of work in mind some of the more progressive schools are now offering a two-year course in Bible, Theology, Comparative Religions, etc., leading to a new degree known as Master of Arts in Religion. (2) Today's emphasis in the homeland on the role of the laity in Christian witness and worship is bound to encourage church members to think in similar terms with regard to overseas service. More and more churches, including the Roman Catholic Church, are experimenting with lay leadership and congregational participation in church services. If laymen can be persuaded to get involved in Christian service at home, they will find it easy to do the same overseas.

Today there are millions of Americans traveling and residing overseas. If all the dedicated Christians among them could be trained and persuaded to be effective witnesses for Jesus Christ, they would add a whole new dimension to the missionary movement. The spiritual potential here is enormous.

In the years ahead there will doubtless be more emphasis on evangelistic missions and less on medical and educational missions. The reason for this is that the governments in the Third World have nationalized most of the mission schools and are now in the process of doing the same with the hospitals. This is a move in the right direction. It is what the colonial governments should have done long ago but didn't. This will set the missionaries free to give more time, thought, energy, and money to the supreme task of "making disciples," which includes gospel preaching, church planting, theological education, Bible translation and revision, literature production and distribution, and mass communications, all of which contribute directly to the building up of the church and the extension of the kingdom. After all, that is what missions is all about. In the past we had no choice; we had to provide educational and medical facilities, first for our converts and later on for the public in general. This day is fast passing, and we should rejoice in our new-found freedom. Now we can concentrate on the job for which we are best qualified.

In the future we can look forward to more inter-mission cooperation on the part of evangelical boards. In the past there has been a tendency for each mission to do its own thing, and this has resulted in a certain amount of duplication and overlapping. This is particularly true in the area of theological education. Each mission wants to run its own Bible school to make sure its pastors and evangelists come out with the right "stamp" on them. In some countries there are twenty or thirty small, struggling Bible schools, each with a handful of students. There are indications that mission leaders are becoming aware of the problem and are prepared to do something about it. A classic example is Union Biblical Seminary in Yeotmal, India, which began in 1938 as a small Free Methodist school, but today is supported by some nineteen mission boards, all of them thoroughly evangelical.

It may even be that some mission mergers will take place. Several of them have already occurred; but in each case the prime consideration was financial. A small mission, rather than cease to exist, has requested to be taken over by a larger mission with more assets and personnel. In evangelical ranks there has been only one merger involving two viable missions on the basis of economy and efficiency of operation. Perhaps it is still too early to expect this kind of merger; but doubtless it will come before long. Between 1973 and 1976 seven mergers were reported among North American mission boards.

Denominational boards, of course, cannot merge with other boards unless and until the denominations themselves merge. Several mergers of this kind have taken place. The interdenominational missions are the ones that have the greatest difficulties. Each mission has its own history, tradition, image, constituency, and membership to think of; and the older the mission, the more cherished these things are.

Saturation evangelism and other forms of inter-mission cooperation are on the increase, and we shall see more of this in the future. If cooperation is desirable at home it is even more essential on the mission field. In two or three countries several missions have pooled their resources and have operated under one banner. The classic example of this kind of cooperation is the United Mission to Nepal, which comprises some thirty different mission boards all operating under one umbrella in Nepal. Another example is the International Afghan Mission.

In the past Roman Catholic and Protestant missions went their separate ways. In most parts of the world there was mutual hostility and opposition. In Latin America the Protestants were openly persecuted by the Roman Catholics. Since Vatican II this has all changed. The Roman Catholic Church is now actively cooperating with the United Bible Societies. Most of the Bible translation and revision now going on is being done by joint committees of Roman Catholics and Protestants. The Bibles are known as union Bibles, acceptable to both sides. The Apocryphal Books are included in the Bibles used by the Catholics, but always at their request and expense. This kind of cooperation was made possible by the decision of the Vatican to give the Bible for the first time to the laymen in the church.

The present openness of the Roman Catholic authorities in Latin America would have been unbelievable fifteen short years ago. Today gospel films produced by the Billy Graham Evangelistic Association and the Moody Institute of Science are being shown in Catholic schools and churches throughout Latin America.

Nowhere has inter-mission cooperation been more widespread than in Bible translation work. In the past four Bible societies carried the lion's share of Bible translation and publication: the British and Foreign Bible Society, the American Bible Society, the National Bible Society of Scotland, and the Netherlands Bible Society. In 1946 the United Bible Societies came into being. Today it has sixty-six member societies, all contributing in their own way to the translation and publication of the Scriptures in over 1,700 languages of the world. Wycliffe Bible Translators, which has translated portions of the Scriptures into over six hundred languages, cooperates with the United Bible Societies in virtually every area of the world. At present well over 75 percent of all Bible translation and publication is being done under the auspices of the UBS or in cooperation with them, cooperation that missions in general might well emulate.

In the past the task of world evangelization rested on the churches of the West. It was taken for granted that this was part of the "white man's burden." In recent years a change has taken place. The "younger" churches of the Third World are beginning to take responsibility for the evangelization of the unreached peoples in their own countries and overseas. Indeed, some of them have sent missionaries to the so-called Christian countries of the West. Hard statistics are difficult to obtain, but reliable estimates indicate that well over three thousand missionaries are now being supported by the churches in the Third World. This is only a beginning. In the future we shall see a great expansion of this kind of missionary interest and outreach. One gets the impression that the "younger" churches are quite excited about the prospect of missionary work around the world. There is every indication that they intend to accept their full share of responsibility for world evangelization. With the rising standard of living in the Third World many of these churches now have the financial base for such an undertaking. This is especially true of the churches in the Far East.

In a pluralistic world it is becoming increasingly difficult for the Christian missionary to insist on the uniqueness of the Christian faith and the finality of Jesus Christ. This is occasioned by two factors: the increasing popularity of relativism in the West and the resurgence of the non-Christian religions of the East. In view of these two developments the missionary is going to look more and more like a relic of bygone days. If there are no absolutes in the moral realm, it is foolish to insist that one religion is true and all the other religions are in varying degrees false. Such a notion is equally repugnant in East and West. We always thought of the nineteenth-century missionary as being a person of great courage. The missionary of the future will need even more courage, but it will be moral rather than physical courage. It is embarrassing to live in a "global village" and insist that the neighbors' gods are false, especially when the neighbors are such fine folks.

Out of this situation grows a demand for dialogue. In the past the preaching of the gospel took the form of monologue. The missionary did all the talking; the others sat and listened, or they quietly walked away. That day has gone. The people in the Third World are not as docile as they once were. They have learned to stand on their own feet and to think for themselves. They are no longer content to listen. They have something to say and they want to be heard.

The devotees of the Eastern religions are by no means persuaded that theirs is a lost cause. Also, they know enough about the moral bankruptcy of the West to have grave misgivings about the "superiority" of the Christian religion. They are still willing to listen to the claims of Christianity as expounded by the missionary, but with the expectation that the missionary will return the compliment and listen to them as they explain the claims of Hinduism, Buddhism, or Islam, as the case may be.

Dialogue has its advantages as well as its disadvantages, especially in the Muslim world. To engage in this kind of dialogue will require great tact, skill, understanding, and love on the part of the missionary. More than ever it will be necessary for him to be well versed in the major doctrines of the great ethnic religions as well as in the Christian Scriptures. It cannot be said too often: it is an act of consummate folly to go to the mission field without an understanding of the non-Christian religions. Indeed, if we at home want to hold our own against the inroads made by Hare Krishna, Soka Gakkai, and Transcendental Meditation, we had better take seriously the study of the Eastern religions.

One of the most hopeful signs on the horizon is the growing strength of the national churches in the Third World; but their very strength has posed serious problems that call for solution. It is no exaggeration to say that church-mission tension in many parts of the world is at an all-time high.

The problem stems in part from the colonial image that still clings to the sending missions of the West. It will be some time before they can live down the reputation of the past. Part of the problem lies with the receiving churches, which have not yet learned to cope with the problems of independence. In a matter of a few years they have gone from the complete dependence of childhood to the bewildering independence of adolescence. This second period is always turbulent; but hopefully it leads on to the interdependence of adulthood. In the meantime the "mother" missions are having a hard time trying to live with the "daughter" churches as they pass through the trial-and-error period of adolescence on their way to the full maturity of adulthood.

Naturally there is some distrust, even suspicion, on both sides, due largely to misunderstanding. If the distrust is to be eliminated there must be dialogue. If dialogue is to be fruitful there must be openness and honesty on both sides. This kind of honest openness will not come overnight. It will have to be cultivated over a period of time. Naturally, the missions should take the initiative. They should encourage the churches to speak their mind without fear of retaliation. There is still a fear in some quarters that funds may be cut off if the churches become too free in their speech. In such circumstances genuine dialogue is impossible. The churches must be persuaded that the missions are sincere in their desire for harmonious dialogue.

Another problem that must be solved in the near future is this: How can the sending missions best help the national churches to develop missionary strategy and structures as they move out to evangelize the unreached peoples of the world? So important is this question that a special study conference was convened in Overland, Kansas, in November 1973, to discuss the matter. Five or six leaders from the national churches were on hand to present their point of view.

It was agreed that the Western missions should stand ready to assist the Third World sending agencies if such assistance is requested. Cooperation between the two groups may or may not be desirable, depending on the needs and attitudes of the Third World leaders. We in the West should not assume that they need our help. It should be given only if requested. If requested, it should be given wisely, in a way that will not do injury to their authentic selfhood. In such instances the paramount authority should reside in the Third World sending agencies. We can easily do more harm than good if we insist on our patterns of work, or impose our organizational structures and financial policies, or become too generous with our money.

As more and more churches in the Third World achieve full maturity the sending missions will have to decide what relationship they will sustain to these churches. There are three possibilities: parallelism, partnership, and fusion. Many of the mainline denominations have already settled for fusion. Their missionaries are now known as "fraternal workers" and are under the supervision and control of the national church. The mission structure has been dismantled, except for the home end of the work.

The evangelical missions hesitate to go that far. They prefer either parallelism or partnership. In parallelism both the sending mission and the receiving church maintain their own work side by side, the one supplementing and complementing the other. In partnership the sending mission and the receiving church agree to work in close collaboration, with missionaries and national leaders sitting together on the same boards and administering joint programs to achieve common goals.

Whichever plan is adopted it is absolutely imperative that the national leaders be in on the decision-making. Otherwise all our fine talk about cooperation is meaningless. The time has come to recognize the full autonomy of the national churches and to treat their leaders as equals in every sense of the word. Tokenism is not good enough.

The sending missions must never forget that they are *missionary* agencies and as such are irrevocably committed to the evangelization of the world. They must never lose this vision or permit the cooperating national churches to forget it. Churches the world over have a tendency, especially in the second and third generations, to lose their first love and their evangelistic zeal and settle down to a comfortable existence with little or no concern for the fate of the unsaved.

Another trend has to do with indigenous theology which is developing in the Third World. Biblical theology is rooted in the Word of God and consequently has nothing to do with East or West *per se*. As it has developed in the West, however, it has acquired certain cultural overtones that have little if any relevance in the Third World. At the same time it is recognized that our theology is what we derive from the Scriptures, and that a Biblical theology is effective in any culture only in the measure in which it is expressed in concepts and terms that are relevant to the needs and aspirations of that culture.

An essential task of the church, therefore, is the careful study of the Scriptures in the context of the culture in which they are to be communicated and the development of a theology that can be successfully communicated to that culture. For such a task the help of Western missionary theologians is both needed and wanted in the Third World, provided they have some knowledge of cross-cultural communications and have lived long enough in the culture to understand and appreciate the nuances of that culture. There is probably no greater service that we can render to the emerging churches in the Third World. Alas, so few missionaries are theologians, and so few theologians are missionaries.

The greatest single focal point of friction between the sending missions and the receiving churches involves the use of foreign funds. The national church leaders have three gripes: (1) The missionary standard of living is usually considerably higher than that of the national worker. (2) Missions are willing to invest money in a given program so long as the missionary is on hand to supervise the use of funds; but when for any reason the missionary is removed the funds are withdrawn. In other words, the money is used to support the person (who is temporary), not the office (which is permanent). (3)

When foreign funds are given to the churches they usually have strings attached.

If church-mission tension is ever to be eliminated some way must be found to defuse this explosive issue. In years past the sending missions used foreign funds all too freely to the detriment of the developing churches. Now the pendulum is in danger of swinging to the opposite extreme and the churches are suddenly told they must sink or swim.

Some missions have done a better job than others. The Christian and Missionary Alliance has in the last decade achieved a remarkably harmonious working relationship with its overseas "daughter" churches, now really "sister" churches. They have settled for the partnership plan and have used foreign funds, not to support local churches and pastors, but as a catalyst to spark missionary giving and vision on the part of church leaders. Today the C&MA churches in Asia have their own missionaries, sent out by their own churches, and supported by their own funds.

There is a growing awareness among mission leaders that while the receiving churches should be fully self-supporting at the local level, there is justification for the use of foreign funds at higher levels of administration. Theological education, certainly at the graduate level, is very costly and in some countries quite beyond the financial capability of the local churches. The evangelical churches of Africa and Madagascar now have a continent-wide association with a full-time executive secretary. The present budget of fifty thousand dollars a year, modest though it is, is a big drain on the meager resources of the national fellowships that compose its membership. For the time being Western funds are being used to help underwrite the program. This seems to be a wise use of foreign funds.

The role of the missionary is changing rapidly. In the heyday of colonialism he was a person of stature, a force to be reckoned with. At home he was a hero; on the field he was a leader. Now he is neither hero nor leader, but just a plain servant. This is a good thing, for it forces the missionary to come to grips with the words of the Master: "As the Father has sent me, even so I send you" (Jn 20:21). And we all know that Jesus Christ came not to be ministered unto but to minister, and to give His life a ransom for many (Mt 20:28).

Seldom in history have the followers of Christ rushed to fill the servant role. Like the early disciples, they have jostled for position and hankered after power. Few of them have taken kindly to the foot-washing ministry commanded by our Lord (Jn 13:14).

Indeed, the role is changing. Yesterday the missionary was the leader. Today he is the partner. Tomorrow he will be the servant.

Opposing Forces

We are living in days of unprecedented opportunities; but along with the opportunities are opposing forces. This should not surprise us. The apostle Paul found the same thing true in his day. He said, "A wide door for effective work has opened to me, and there are many adversaries" (1 Co 16:9). Our Lord said as much when He sent out the twelve apostles: "Behold, I send you out as sheep in the midst of wolves. . . . Beware of men; for they will deliver you up to councils, and flog you in their synagogues, and you will be dragged before governors and kings for my sake" (Mt 10:16-18).

Mao Tse-tung, the greatest revolutionist of the twentieth century, said on one occasion that a revolution is not a tea party. Neither is the missionary enterprise. Missionary work has always involved all kinds of difficulties and dangers. As it was in the past, so it will be in the future. Opposing forces should not discourage or deter us; rather they should spur us on to greater effort.

Some of these opposing forces operate right here in the homeland; others are encountered only on the field. But whether here or there they are formidable foes of the gospel and should be recognized as such. Before moving on to the mission field we shall discuss certain obstacles in the homeland that militate against the worldwide Christian mission.

The first of these would have to be the moral decadence of Western civilization. The distinction between Christendom and heathendom, so marked in the nineteenth century, is rapidly disappearing. Europe is no longer a Christian continent; and North America is rapidly going down the same road. Western culture is becoming less and less Christian in its content. In fact we ourselves are now talking of a "post-Christian era." And well we might.

Our large metropolitan centers are controlled by gangsters. Our inner cities are jungles of violence and crime. Our entire political system, including the police and the courts, is honeycombed with corruption. X-rated movies and pornographic literature are flooding our sex-saturated society. Premarital sex, adultery, abortion (new name for infanticide), prostitution, divorce, cheating, shoplifting, and gambling —all have reached unprecedented heights in the past ten years. Less "sinful" but equally reprehensible have been our love of money, our penchant for war, our pursuit of happiness, and our preoccupation with material prosperity.

Fifty years ago the peoples of the Third World knew the United States largely through the missionaries residing in those parts. To this day they assume that all Americans are Christians. Now with worldwide, instantaneous mass communications, Uncle Sam (sometimes called Uncle Sham) stands naked and ugly before the non-Christian world.

It is a shame, but we must confess that the moral standards in the non-Christian countries are often higher than in our own. Many of the governments have taken action to keep out the various forms of pollution from the West. The most puritanical society in today's world is Communist China, which has abolished both God and religion.

All this makes it increasingly difficult for the Western missionary to preach the gospel in the Third World. They argue that if Christianity has failed so miserably in the West why should it be exported to the East? They can be forgiven if they say to the missionary: "Physician, heal thyself."

Particularly vexatious is the problem of racial prejudice in the United States. We are not the only country to have this problem; but we are the largest, strongest, and best known; and what we say and do today is prominently displayed in the world headlines tomorrow. We are indeed a city that is set on a hill and cannot be hid (Mt 5:14), which adds to the gravity of the situation.

If segregation were confined to American society it would be bad enough, but it is found in the Christian churches as well. Indeed the most segregated hour of the week is between eleven and twelve o'clock on Sunday morning. African Christians visiting this country have been mistaken for Afro-Americans and treated as second-class citizens, even by the churches. When the error is discovered profuse apologies are offered; but the damage has been done. There is no doubt about it; racial prejudice in this country is a millstone around the neck of the missionary in the Third World.

The assassination of President Kennedy and his brother Bobby and Martin Luther King, all within a few years, shocked not only the American people but the people of the entire world. In every country American missionaries were bombarded with a barrage of questions, some of them quite hostile. How could a so-called Christian nation descend to such barbarity? Needless to say, the missionaries had no satisfactory answers.

Following the death of Dr. King, Jack Robinson, missionary in Senegal, wrote: "We have sensed real cooling off in the attitude of the people since our arrival in Senegal three years ago because of the reports they get of the horrible racial situation in the United States. Many have the impression that our whole country is burning. Being an American is no longer to our advantage."[1]

And what shall be said of the Vietnam War, the longest and dirti-

---

[1] Jack Robinson, *Impact* (February 1969), p. 7.

est in our history? Fortunately the war is over—at least so far as Americans are concerned—and people have short memories, so the whole mess will soon be forgotten. But while it lasted it was a constant source of embarrassment to American missionaries overseas. Here again the missionaries were hard pressed for an explanation that would satisfy the questioners.

The presence of hundreds of thousands of American GIs overseas has done nothing to enhance the image of "Christian" America in the eyes of the Third World. Besides getting into drunken brawls and otherwise making a nuisance of themselves, the GIs in Japan, Korea, and Vietnam sired thousands of babies. Deserted by their fathers, unwanted by their mothers, and unable to hide their identity, these children are the most unfortunate in the world. World Vision International, the Pearl Buck Foundation, and other similar organizations have done what they could to alleviate the situation; but the problem was much too great for their meager resources. As long as they live these victims of modern warfare will carry with them the stigma of their origin.

Another developing force is neo-isolationism. Isolationism was the official policy of the United States between the two world wars. Following World War II the United States, through no fault of its own, had to assume the leadership of the free world. Our most successful venture was the Marshall Plan, that put Western Europe back on its feet and checked the advance of Communist power in that part of the world. President Truman's Point Four Plan was likewise very successful, for it kept Greece and Turkey from falling into the Russian orbit. In the last twenty-five years our foreign aid program has cost the American taxpayer over 100 billion dollars, and this does not include the enormously costly Vietnam War.

And what do we have to show for our generosity? Not very much. A good deal of our foreign aid found its way into the black markets that developed overseas. Some of it ended up in the pockets of the politicians. In the process we made as many enemies as friends. Now with mounting problems at home the American people are asking, "Why give to others when we don't have enough money for ourselves?" "Is it not time to put our own house in order?" This is what Senator McGovern had in mind when he closed his acceptance speech at the 1972 Democratic Convention with the plea, "Come home, America." A growing number of Americans are disillusioned with the United Nations and advocate that we pull out. In the United States Congress there is a growing sentiment in favor of withdrawing American troops from Europe. We are determined never again to get our fingers burned in overseas operations. This kind of "me first" psychology makes a strong appeal to the innate selfishness of human nature.

If this mood becomes widespread, it could easily have an adverse effect on Christian missions, for, whether we like to admit it or not, the church usually is only five or ten years behind the world. If the American government decides to abdicate its worldwide responsibilities the American church might well do the same with its worldwide missionary enterprise.

Another opposing force is the resurgence of the great non-Christian religions of Asia. Fifty years ago missionaries on furlough spoke hopefully of the breakup of the ethnic religions. No one talks that way today. With the advent of independence these religions have taken a new lease on life and are passing from the defensive to the offensive. Throughout the entire Muslim world the study of Islam is a required subject in all public schools from grade school through university. New mosques are being built and old ones are being refurbished; and attendance is on the increase. A missionary in Tunis in 1973 wrote: "A trend to more strict observance of Islam is noticeable, and it is common to see women and men, young and old, attending prayers at the mosques, whereas 10 years ago prayers were considered 'for mice and old men.' " Today there are 25 million Muslims in Europe.

In India Hinduism is making a valiant effort to win back the hundreds of thousands of converts (former untouchables) lost to Christianity. Some of the more militant Hindus are calling for the expulsion of all missionaries. Two state governments were persuaded to pass anti-conversion laws; they were later struck down by the Supreme Court as unconstitutional. The Bhagavad-Gita has been translated into hundreds of languages, and a cheap paperback edition in English can be purchased in the corner drug store on Main Street, U.S.A. The Hare Krishna Movement, Transcendental Meditation, and Eastern Mysticism, all from India, are now invading the West and sweeping thousands of American youth off their feet. Buddhism, known through the centuries for its emphasis on meditation, has suddenly become both missionary and militant. In South Vietnam Buddhist monks helped to topple more than one Saigon regime during the 1960s. Buddhist scriptures are being translated into the major languages of Europe and Buddhist missionaries are to be found in all parts of the Western world. Outside the international airport in Colombo there is a huge poster exhorting the people to contribute money to send Buddhist missionaries to Europe.

Soka Gakkai in Japan, combining prayer and politics, has won over ten million families since 1950. Its religious exclusiveness, militant nationalism, forced conversions, political ambitions, and worldwide missionary aims make it Christianity's most formidable foe in Japan. More recently it has invaded the West, where it is making converts in significant numbers. Writing in the English-language *Seikyo Times* its leader, Mr. Ikeda, said: "We have a message! We are committed to the salvation of mankind. Our aim is to save the masses from misfortune and misery and to establish a happy life for every individual. We must create a peaceful world. Soka Gakkai is not only the hope of Japan, but the hope of the world."

Another opposing force that is gathering momentum today is syncretism. Visser't Hooft defines syncretism as "the view which holds that there is no unique revelation in history, that there are many ways to reach the divine reality, that all formulations of religious truth or experience are by their very nature inadequate expressions of that truth and that it is necessary to harmonize as much as possible all religious ideas and experiences so as to create one universal religion for mankind."[2]

This point of view is gaining wide acceptance in both East and West. The Vedanta school of thought in Hinduism maintains that it is possible to realize God by various ways—Jesus, Krishna, Mohammed, Zoroaster, and others. Gandhi said the same. Arnold Toynbee castigates Christianity for its "arrogance" and predicts that unless it rids itself of its exclusive spirit it will be rejected by modern man—East and West. He prefers to believe that "all the higher religions are also revelations of what is true and right. They also come from God and each presents some facet of God's truth."[3]

This problem has been with us for a long time, but it is particularly acute in these days when the national churches in the Third World are trying to make Christianity indigenous to the national culture. The Indian church wants to make Christianity indigenous to India and the African church wants to do the same in Africa. This is good and proper. This is what the early church did with Christianity in the Graeco-Roman world. But there is a serious problem: How far can the process of indigenization go without altering the hard core of Christian doctrine and practice?

Nowhere is the problem greater than in Africa, where some seven thousand independent churches (denominations) are trying to develop an African form of Christianity. Many of these churches are a strange mixture of animism, native customs, and magic, with certain Christian elements added and the whole embellished with the external symbols of Christianity. "Among the many independent churches and sects which have grown up in Africa there are those which simply seek to give a more specifically Christian [African] expression to the Christian faith without departing from that faith. But there are others which

2 W. A. Visser't Hooft, No Other Name (Philadelphia: Westminster Press, 1963), p. 11.
3 Arnold Toynbee, Christianity Among the Religions of the World (New York: Charles Scribner's Sons, 1957), pp. 99-100.

have gone so far in reintroducing traditional African religious ideas and practices (sometimes including magic) that they have become essentially syncretistic."[4]

The missionary finds himself in a very delicate situation. If he does nothing and allows the church to lapse into baptized paganism, he will be abdicating his responsibility. If he tries to point out the dangers inherent in the situation he may be accused of "theological imperialism." In either case he is in trouble. This is one reason why the evangelical missions should help to train national theologians, who will be able to cope with the problem better than we can.

Another opposing force is nationalism. It is common knowledge that nationalism has been the greatest force in the Third World during most of the twentieth century. With the achievement of independence nationalism has a way of cooling off. Though the most turbulent phase is probably over it is by no means dead. With the passing of time nationalism will gradually give way to internationalism; but we still have a long way to go before we reach that stage. Inasmuch as nationalism is directed against outsiders and all missionaries are expatriates, it stands to reason that nationalism will pose a problem for years to come.

Now that these countries are sovereign, independent states they have every right to order their internal affairs and their foreign policies as they see fit. Their immigration authorities have a perfect right to exclude or expel anyone they consider undesirable. All foreigners are now guests; as such they enter, remain, and depart only with permission of the government. They have no rights, only privileges. This is in stark contrast to colonial times when the missionaries came and went and did as they liked.

To make matters worse many of these countries are under military dictatorships of the left or the right, which means that civil and political rights are shelved for the time being. Many of them have demographic and economic problems—too many people and too few jobs. Such governments do not want expatriates taking jobs away from their own citizens. Some governments, such as in Thailand, impose an annual quota on the number of foreigners to whom they will give permanent residence visas. Other governments will accept only citizens from "friendly" countries. Still other governments, such as Burma, are determined to get rid of all expatriates.

In the "good old days" all that missionaries needed was a passport; and British missionaries going to British colonies didn't need even that. Today they need work permits in addition to passports and visas if they want to remain in the country longer than the usual time

---

[4] Visser't Hooft, *op. cit.*, p. 45.

allotted to tourists. In some countries these are difficult to obtain; and once obtained, they have to be renewed every year or two. Missionaries without a residence permit are treated like tourists and have to leave the country every month or so to have their permits renewed. They usually step over the border into a neighboring country, spend a day or two there, do some shopping or sightseeing, and return within forty-eight hours. This procedure, of course, is costly in time and money.

Many countries now require a work permit for all aliens holding a residence permit. This is even harder to get because of the high rate of unemployment in many of the underdeveloped countries. In some instances the applications get lost in the bureaucratic red tape while the missionaries wait patiently—or impatiently—for their permits. In 1973 some three hundred visas for missionaries going to Brazil were held up because of an interdepartmental feud between the Foreign Office and the Ministry of Labor. If the apostle Paul had encountered this kind of problem he would not have been able to support himself and his colleagues by tent-making.

Bernard Shaw once said that nationalism is like a cancer and when a person has cancer he can think of nothing else. This seems to be the case with certain dictators and demagogues who have seized power in recent years. Independence has produced a whole crop of politicians more interested in their own self-aggrandizement than in the welfare of the people. They build magnificent presidential palaces, surround themselves and their cronies with a platoon of bodyguards, outlaw all opposition parties, declare martial law, impose censorship on the press and radio, and apply various kinds of pressure on minority groups, especially aliens.

In 1973 President Amin of Uganda gave forty thousand Asians ninety days to leave the country; and they were not permitted to take their money with them. About the same time he outlawed twelve "religious sects" declared to be "dangerous to peace and order." Earlier fifty-eight missionaries were expelled, accused of having "entered the country illegally, were qualified military men dressed in religious habits and yet could not answer questions about the Bible."[5]

In Zaire President Mobutu is throwing his weight around. During 1973 he expelled the Roman Catholic cardinal, forced Christians to adopt Zairean names, and outlawed all uniformed youth groups, church business meetings, and religious periodicals. His actions were directed against the growing power of the Roman Catholic hierarchy; but Protestants were naturally included in all the directives.

In the past year several Muslim countries have cracked down on missionary activities. In Afghanistan the only church in the country

---

[5] *Afroscope* (November 1973), p. 3.

was bulldozed by order of the government, and half a dozen non-professional missionaries under the International Afghan Mission were expelled with no reason given for the action. Somalia opened to missionary work in 1954 but closed again in 1973. Iran closed in 1981.

Another opposing force is Communism. Communism is not the monolithic world structure we once thought it to be. Nor does it pose the same threat to world peace as it did in the fifties and sixties. Moreover the détente between the USSR and the United States and the exchange of diplomatic personnel between Communist China and the United States have resulted in a relaxed atmosphere. It is doubtful, however, if either the Soviet Union or Communist China has given up its ultimate goal of world revolution. In the 1960s both countries overplayed their hands in certain parts of the world and suffered embarrassing setbacks as a result. Both countries are actively engaged in extending their influence in certain strategic regions, the Russians in the Middle East and Africa, and the Chinese in Asia.

Marxist regimes have already emerged in Angola and Mozambique; as a result both church and mission work have suffered. After South Yemen turned Communist several years ago mission property was confiscated and all missionaries were expelled. South Vietnam, after many years of attack and infiltration from the North, fell under Communist control in April 1975, despite the prior involvement of Western nations. As predicted, missionary work there has come to an abrupt halt, and church leaders have gone to prison.

There is another opposing force the full extent of which is not yet known. This is the high cost of missionary work. The American people are rightly concerned about the rate of inflation in our economy; at least we can derive comfort from the fact that it is lower in the United States than in other industrialized states. And if we think it is bad in Europe, it is many times worse in other parts of the world. In some countries the cost of living soars as much as 100 percent a year. In Chile inflation ran wild in 1973, rising almost 400 percent in the first six months!

Added to inflation abroad have been two devaluations of the American dollar, amounting to almost 20 percent. The inflation in Japan coupled with the devaluation of the American dollar reduced the purchasing power of the missionary's remittance by over 40 percent. In Japan steak runs as high as fifteen dollars a pound and an eight-ounce glass of orange juice costs three dollars. If it is true that "a day without orange juice is like a day without sunshine," the missionaries in Japan do not enjoy much sunshine!

Some governments are now trying to squeeze every dollar they can out of foreigners passing through or residing in their countries. Singapore has recently passed a law requiring all persons, including students, entering the country to make a deposit of $3,000. Jordan demands as much as $4,000 duty on a secondhand car and a $350 license fee. Some countries levy a head tax on everyone entering or leaving the country. Many, taking their cue from the West, have introduced the personal income tax; and missionaries along with other expatriates have to pay up. Others go so far as to charge duty on medical and relief supplies furnished free by missionary and humanitarian agencies in the West.

What shall be said about the price of land and buildings? In some countries the sky is the limit. Japan heads the list. In residential areas land costs $1.2 million per acre. To build even a small church on $\frac{1}{25}$ of an acre costs well over $100,000. Land prices in some of the larger cities, like Osaka and Nagoya, have been known to jump 200 to 300 percent in a single year.[6] Needless to say, mission boards don't have that kind of money. The problem could be solved by renting instead of buying; but rents are not cheap either. In some cities missionaries are paying $500 to $700 a month for a small apartment.

There is no doubt about it. The missionary enterprise is now a costly business; and unless the churches in this country get behind it and support it up to the hilt, there is bound to be a certain amount of retrenchment over the next decade. One mission board with fewer than seventy missionaries reckons that an extra $150,000 a year will be needed to maintain its present missionary force. Recently the author received a year-end letter from a mission asking for $53,000 to enable it to end the year in the black. During the past year some churches failed to meet their commitments to the missionaries; so the mission "borrowed" from other funds to prevent undue hardship on the part of the missionaries. Now these funds have to be replenished. Scores of letters of this kind come to the author's desk every December.

When 220 leaders of the United Bible Societies met in Thailand in December 1980 they stated that the major factor holding up the distribution of the Scriptures is not closing doors, hostile regimes, or civil wars but the shortage of funds. During the 1980s they anticipate a shortfall of $7 million. Other organizations have the same problem, and with many countries experiencing recession, the situation will persist.

Unlimited Opportunities

As indicated in the preceding section the Christian mission in this postcolonial period is facing many opposing forces. At the same time

---

[6]*The Evangelical Beacon*, August 1, 1981, p. 18.

there are unprecedented opportunities; and the former should not be allowed to obscure the latter.

It is true that missionaries have a hard time getting into some countries and after they get there they have to endure petty annoyances of one kind or another; but upon their arrival they usually find the people friendly. Most of the ill will, mistrust, suspicion, and animosity that exist in the world today have been generated not by peoples but by governments. They are the ones that make laws, break treaties, and declare war. Trade barriers, immigration quotas, and other obstacles designed to keep the nations apart are established by the politicians, not the people. When people are left to themselves they usually manage to get along pretty well with other people.

When the missionary gets into a foreign country he invariably finds the people open and friendly on a person-to-person basis. For all the anti-American propaganda that was generated by the Cold War there is still an enormous reservoir of good will for the United States. It is no exaggeration to say that in spite of all our faults and failings America enjoys the confidence and admiration of most of the world. It is noteworthy in this connection that our two former enemies, Germany and Japan, both of whom we reduced to rubble, are today our strongest allies. When the chips are down even the Arabs in the Middle East prefer to do business with us rather than with the USSR, and that in spite of our consistent support of the State of Israel. This is not intended as a pat on the back for Uncle Sam; it is simply a recognition of the facts in international life.

In spite of administrative red tape many governments in the Third World are coming to see that the missionaries are their best friends and they are still willing to give them preferential treatment. The government of Thailand is urging religious leaders and missionaries to help solve some of the nation's problems. The country's new Alien Occupation Law, which restricts the practice of some fifty-eight occupations to Thai nationals, does not apply to teachers of religion. Missionaries have been told that the government considers their work beneficial to the country. They have been urged to win those committed to no faith and to "try to win the hearts of the young people."

David Wilkerson, during a recent crusade in Brazil, was invited to speak to the Legislative Assembly in session in Sao Paulo. The governor and other key officials met with him privately to discuss ways and means of combatting the growing drug problem. In every city that he visited, Wilkerson was swarmed by reporters seeking interviews regarding the critical youth problems now facing Brazil. The nation's largest leading magazine, *Manchete*, featured his crusades.

In country after country churches and missions are being given prime time on national networks for religious programs. The Africa Inland Mission produces over a hundred programs a month for broadcast over the powerful government station in Nairobi. In Zambia President Kenneth Kaunda has given the churches as much radio time on the national network as they are able to program. Each Sunday evening Monrovia's only television station telecasts a program, "New Life in Christ," prepared by the Sudan Interior Mission.

The government of Kenya recently gave the Assemblies of God a beautiful piece of property worth $100,000 in the most densely populated part of Nairobi. An influential Ethiopian offered the Sudan Interior Mission a tract of land if it could find the manpower to develop a mission center. Alas, the offer had to be turned down for lack of personnel. In Paraguay the Ministry of National Education recently gave permission for the Bible Society to place Scriptures in the hands of every school and college student in the country.

Far from wanting to get rid of the missionaries, some governments have recently gone out of their way to honor their work. The government of Korea has issued a commemorative postage stamp honoring World Vision for twenty years of child care and other forms of social service. The government of Liberia has conferred a similar honor on the Sudan Interior Mission. A special commemorative postage stamp was issued on January 18, 1974, to mark the twentieth anniversary of Radio Station ELWA. Two medical missionaries, Titus Johnson and Arden Almquist, on the staff of the Paul Carlson Medical Center in Zaire, were decorated by the government with the highest medal of honor for their "distinguished service to the nation." On August 31, 1973, Wycliffe Bible Translators in the Philippines received the Ramon Magsaysay Award for International Understanding, widely regarded as the Asian equivalent of the Nobel Peace Prize.

The missionary may have lost some of his glamor among his friends at home. He is still making a solid contribution overseas where his presence is appreciated by those who see him in action.

C. Stacey Woods, former General Secretary of the International Fellowship of Evangelical Students, writing in 1972, said;

> I see two worldwide, contradictory crosscurrents strongly flowing: First, there is the rushing torrent of godlessness, sensuality, secularism and violence, which is increasing everywhere. Second, there is what many of us believe may be the final great movement of God's Spirit just before the Day of God's grace ends and the awesome Day of the Lord begins. This is seen most significantly in the tremendous increase in the study of God's Word. Second, in the many movements worldwide, which are being used of God in the salvation of young and old.[7]

---

7 C. Stacey Woods, *Asia Pulse*, Vol. III, No. 3 (April 1972), p. 101.

There is no doubt that the Spirit of God in our day is working in strange ways and in most unexpected places. It is literally a worldwide movement embracing Christians and non-Christians alike, renewing the one and converting the other. The churches at home are being renewed and the churches overseas are growing by leaps and bounds, some of them doubling and tripling their total membership in the last decade.

After his 1973 crusade in Korea, attended by 4.5 million people, Billy Graham said, "I seriously doubt if my own ministry can ever be the same again." Dr. Myron Augsburger, President of Eastern Mennonite College, after a recent world tour said that he is convinced that the Third World is the cutting edge of the Christian church today. All who visit the mission field come back with the same observation. The words *fabulous* and *fantastic* are being used to describe the situation. Millions are turning to the Lord and tens of millions are being exposed to the Christian gospel for the very first time. And this quest for spiritual reality is not confined to the poverty-stricken masses, whose interest in religion might be suspect. It includes teachers, students, government officials, successful businessmen, and others whose hearts have been touched by the Holy Spirit.

Some denominations are finding that their overseas work is expanding so rapidly that the "daughter" churches in the Third World now have a larger cumulative membership than the "mother" church in this country. Among such groups are the Christian and Missionary Alliance, the Assemblies of God, and the Seventh-day Adventists. The Assemblies report 1.3 million members in the U.S.A. In Brazil the membership stands at 6.1 million. The total for the Third World is 12.2 million. In 1980 the Full Gospel Central Church in Seoul gave $6 million to foreign missions.

Mass evangelism seems to have had its day in the homelands. Billy Graham is about the only evangelist who can attract and hold large audiences today. Not so on the mission field. Beginning in 1960 Evangelism-in-Depth brought the small, timid churches of Latin America out of their ghettoes and into the streets, parks, municipal auditoriums, and soccer stadiums for city-wide rallies. From Latin America the idea spread to Africa and Asia, where the program is known by various names: New Life For All (West Africa), Christ For All (Zaire), Evangelism Deep and Wide (South Vietnam), Total Mobilization (Japan), and Christ the Only Way (Philippines). In 1958 the Assemblies of God launched a mass evangelism program known as Good News Crusades. These have been held in scores of large cities in all parts of the world and have resulted in greatly accelerated growth. The Southern Baptists have likewise gone in for huge evangelistic campaigns with gratifying results.

The Argentine evangelist, Luis Palau, has a burden for the 350 million Spanish-speaking people, whom he hopes to reach with the gospel in a ten-year period. He has held crusades in several of the Latin American countries with amazing response on the part of the people. Four crusades in Guatemala attracted 100,000 persons, with 3,000 first-time decisions. In addition, he did simultaneous live talk shows over the nation's three television stations. In Lima, Peru, 103,000 persons attended the meetings in the Bull Ring. Over 4,500 indicated their decision to follow Christ. During the crusade Palau appeared on television thirteen times with messages, counseling sessions, and talk shows. Forty-five radio stations around the country carried news and excerpts from the crusade. A press conference in downtown Lima was attended by forty-two newsmen. It is estimated that thirty million Latin Americans have seen and heard Palau on television.

Church growth in the Philippines is taking on all the aspects of a prairie fire. In 1970 the All Philippines Congress on Evangelism called for ten thousand evangelistic Bible study groups throughout the country. By March 1973 the goal had been reached. In November 1980, 488 church leaders representing eighty-one denominations and parachurch organizations convened a Congress on Discipling a Nation. The Congress declared its intention to give every citizen in the nation a genuine opportunity to make an intelligent decision about Christ. To accomplish this it will be necessary to have at least one vibrant evangelical congregation in every *barrio*. To achieve this monumental task would mean increasing the ten thousand present congregations to fifty thousand by the year 2000. At the close of the Congress they declared, "We are aware of the immensity of the task, and our frailties humble us, but we move forward in the confidence that in the power of the Holy Spirit His strength is made perfect in our weakness."

In the spring of 1973 French evangelist Jacques Giraud was invited to Ivory Coast for a one-week evangelistic crusade. So powerful were the meetings in the capital, Abidjan, that the city council canceled all sporting events and gave the evangelistic team the use of the huge soccer stadium. Morning and evening for *six* weeks thirty to thirty-five thousand people crowded into the stadium. During the first part of the crusade the evangelist emphasized the power of Christ to heal. Hundreds were healed, including some high government officials and their relatives. By the end of the first week the crusade was the talk of the town. During the second part of the crusade Mr. Giraud emphasized the power of Christ to save. Having already witnessed the healing of the body, the people responded in droves.

In Abidjan over fifteen hundred were baptized. The Bible Society sold out its entire stock: twelve thousand New Testaments, two thousand Bibles, and twenty thousand Gospels. Never in the history of Ivory Coast had so much Christian literature been sold in so short a time.

As the meetings in the capital drew to a close government officials persuaded the evangelist to hold similar meetings in the interior. The minister of state insisted that he go to his hometown, Moumodi, for a week on his way to Bouake where he had been invited by the minister of the interior and the mayor of the city. From that point on the government took care of all arrangements, including hospitality and finances, something previously unheard of in Ivory Coast—or anywhere else.

In November 1972, Dr. Stanley Mooneyham of World Vision, accompanied by Anglican Archbishop Marcus Loane of Australia and Bishop Chandu Ray of Singapore, conducted a city-wide campaign in Phnom Penh, capital of Kampuchea (Cambodia). Every night the twelve-hundred-seat Municipal Music Hall was filled, with an overflow crowd on the closing Sunday. Altogether 2,681 persons publicly expressed their desire to know more about Jesus Christ. Were there any lasting results? The facts speak for themselves. In 1971 the Khmer Evangelical Church had only one congregation in Phnom Penh. By 1975 the number had risen to twenty-seven. Alas, these churches were destroyed when the Communists came to power that same year.

Similar stories of church growth come from all parts of the mission field. Churches are springing up with such rapidity that it is quite impossible adequately to shepherd the flock. The Sudan Interior Mission reports that prior to the civil war in Nigeria the Evangelical Church of West Africa had only four congregations in the Eastern Region, then known as Biafra. Today in that same region there are eighty churches, with over eight thousand people in the Sunday services.

In 1975, a thrilling report came from the Wallamo people in Ethiopia. In a three-month period ten thousand adults renounced their spirit worship. Entire villages turned to Christ. Witch doctors were converted and joined the church. New congregations were growing up so rapidly that the Sudan Interior Mission hardly knew how to cope with the mushroom growth which threatened to get out of hand.

Dr. Clyde W. Taylor, after a visit in Africa, wrote, "In some areas where New Life For All campaigns have been held there has been a 50 percent church growth in one year. The results are fantastic but can only be preserved with thorough follow-up by the churches. This type of evangelism demands the total attention of the church while it lasts."[8] The New Life for All campaign in Central African Republic resulted in a 65 percent church growth in one year.

---

[8] Clyde W. Taylor, *Africa Pulse*, Vol. III, No. 5 (December 1972), p. 3.

And what shall be said about evangelism and church growth in South America? The Pentecostal churches in Brazil are growing at a rate of 20 percent a year. Some twenty-five hundred to three thousand new congregations are being formed there every year.

Even among the Indians of South America, who have proved in the past to be so resistant to the gospel, there is now a gracious moving of the Holy Spirit. The Gospel Missionary Union reports a breakthrough in the evangelization of the Quichua Indians in Ecuador. For over seventy years these descendants of the ancient Incas resisted all attempts at conversion. The first break came in 1967 when 116 professed faith in Christ and were baptized. There are now more than 26,000 baptized believers and many more who are undergoing instruction. In 1973 the American Bible Society published a new translation of the Quichua New Testament. The influence of the Quichua church is being felt in other parts of South America. At least fifteen groups of believers have sprung up in Colombia as a direct result of the evangelistic endeavors of the Quichua believers in Ecuador.

From Bolivia comes word of a similar movement among the Aymara Indians.

> Yesterday (May 15, 1973) I was handed the last report on the Aymara church growth on the Altiplano. It shows tremendous increase, even after the latest figures of February. Forty-one new churches have been raised up in three months! Four hundred and fifty new members have been baptized during the same time. . . . My life and ministry for the Lord will never be the same. Since I have seen the churches growing and expanding throughout the whole country, I will never try to do anything else in my life. Church planting is exciting! And contagious.[9]

Nowhere is Christian missionary work more thrilling than in the student world, where thousands are turning to Christ every year. Students the world over are known for their open-mindedness and their willingness to examine different points of view. More and more of them are becoming disillusioned with their own religions and are willing to examine the claims of Christianity. The International Fellowship of Evangelical Students, with headquarters in London, now has full-time staff workers in sixty-three countries serving forty-nine national member movements, and from all of them except the Muslim world come reports of increased attendance and interest. It is too early to report a breakthrough in student work; but we may be on the threshold of great things.

The General Secretary of IFES writes: "We are working toward the time when hundreds of graduates will cross national and cultural frontiers in obedience to the Lord's missionary mandate to 'go into all

---

[9] Bruno Frigoli, *Church Growth Bulletin*, Vol. IX, No. 6 (July 1973), p. 334.

the world and make disciples of all nations.' "[10] The Christian Union at Oxford University reported the conversion of more than 150 students at its February 1973 mission. That same month a training course was held at Concepción in Chile. The leader reported,

> We've had a glorious manifestation of the Lord's presence at our camp. We expected 40 students to attend and actually 83 turned up! Some non-Christian students, who at first opposed us, met the Lord and were wonderfully converted. These were led to Christ by Christian students. On the day of departure, the Christian students preached the gospel openly at the railway station and some of the listeners professed faith in Christ.[11]

On one occasion, the Reverend John R. W. Stott conducted an evangelical mission at the University of Nairobi. The mission lasted for eight days. The average attendance was six hundred. Each evening students stayed behind and talked until midnight. A thousand students turned out for the closing meeting.

At Ahmadu Bello University in Zaria, Nigeria, the Fellowship of Christian Students organized a four-day evangelistic crusade with a Nigerian pastor as the featured speaker. The crusade theme was "Who Is Jesus?" On the opening night the crusade faced stiff competition from a troupe of dancers and musicians hired for a special party. But the fears of the crusade sponsors proved groundless. Only fifteen turned up for the party and eight of them left early and joined the crusade meeting. An estimated three thousand students were present each of the four nights of the crusade; some two hundred of them stayed for counseling.

If anyone is thinking seriously of going into student work, he or she should give serious consideration to service on the mission field. That's where the action is.

In this connection it is interesting to learn that the leading universities in Sierra Leone, Ghana, Nigeria, Zaire, Uganda, Kenya, and Ethiopia now have important departments in theological disciplines. Qualified missionary-theologians would find a challenging field in any of these universities. That religion has again come into its own on the college campuses of the United States is seen from the fact that two prestigious universities—Stanford and UCLA—have both introduced an undergraduate major in religious studies. Could any professor ask for a more exciting mission field?

Dr. Harold O. J. Brown, former Theological Secretary of the International Fellowship of Evangelical Students, after a tour of the Far East wrote to the dean of a well-known theological seminary in the United States:

---

[10] Chua Wee Hian, *IFES Newsletter*, October 1973.
[11] *IFES Prayer and Praise Bulletin*, April 1973.

There are some very real opportunities for theological teaching, to a large extent in English, in seminaries in all of the countries of South East Asia. . . . In Singapore, Hong Kong, Malaysia, the Philippines, and even Taiwan and Indonesia, there are a number of opportunities for a young man who is willing to devote several years of his life to the task. In many of these places there are relatively under-staffed theological schools facing a tremendous challenge. They have eager students, mostly with a rather low degree of background but with a high level of zeal and often with a tremendous faith. In all of these countries, the educational level and academic aspirations are rising rapidly. People with minimal academic theological training are no longer capable of filling the churches' need in many cases. Perhaps the greatest handicap for the existing evangelical schools is lack of faculty.[12]

That appeal is now ten years old but the need still remains. In fact it is greater than ever. Fully qualified theologians prefer to remain in the States where, so they think, they can have wider scope for their erudition. The need for better-educated pastors in the Third World is ten times greater than it is here at home. The person who goes abroad to teach theology has the satisfaction of knowing that he is filling a role that few other people are qualified to fill. And he will not find anywhere else in the world a more highly motivated group of students. He will be their *guru* and as long as they live they will cherish the memory of his name.

If teaching at the graduate level is too high for many missionaries, there are ample opportunities to teach at the Bible college level. There are hundreds of Bible schools on the mission field and they are always in need of competent, dedicated teachers who love the Lord, know the Word, and have the gift of teaching. Greater Europe Mission now operates ten Bible schools with more to open in the next few years. Total enrollment in these schools now stands at 465, an increase of 20 percent in the last two years. The Assemblies of God maintain 204 Bible schools in 108 countries of the world. Total enrollment is 19,072. Indeed there are very few missions that do not have at least one Bible school. The opportunities here are endless.

Another opportunity, quite unknown in the United States, is the teaching of Religious Knowledge in the government schools in many parts of the Third World. In Anglophone Africa the governments require that all students study religion, either Islam or Christianity. The African churches at this point do not have qualified teachers in sufficient numbers to meet the demand. Hence many missionaries are now employed on the staff of the government schools teaching Christianity and getting paid to do the job.

---

[12] Harold O. J. Brown, *Letter*, January 9, 1970.

Kagoro in Nigeria was for years a large Sudan Interior Mission educational center, with a mission-operated primary school, secondary school, teachers college, and Bible college. The mission now maintains only the Bible college with seven staff members; but it has six missionaries teaching Bible classes full time in the government-administered schools. One of the missionaries was thrilled with her new assignment. She wrote: "I am doing more direct missionary work now than I have done in my sixteen years in Nigeria."[13] Les Greer reports thirty-seven Bible classes a week in the government schools in the city of Kano and more opportunities for personal witness than he can handle. In addition to the Religious Knowledge classes, the teachers are often responsible for baptismal classes, leadership training courses, monthly Communion services, and the promotion of the Fellowship of Christian Students, which has branches in most of the high schools and colleges.

More strategic than teaching Religious Knowledge is the training of student teachers to teach the same subject. In this way the missionary-teacher is multiplying himself many times. A member of the Overseas Missionary Fellowship was asked by the government of Indonesia to prepare a complete syllabus for the teaching of Christianity in the public school system of Indonesia, which is a Muslim country. Another missionary was asked to undertake a similar assignment for the government of South Africa. One could hardly ask for a more strategic ministry.

The government of South Sudan is trying desperately to rehabilitate the devastated countryside after seventeen years of civil war which took tens of thousands of lives and drove at least 250,000 refugees into exile. Word has just been received that the minister of education wants nineteen qualified teachers and administrators to go to South Sudan to help set up several new high schools now on the planning boards. He prefers to have Christians and has asked the missionaries now working under the African Committee for the Rehabilitation of Southern Sudan to recruit them. It remains to be seen whether our Christian young people will rise to the challenge. In the 1960s similar calls came from Nigeria and Kenya, but neither of the two missions asked to do the recruiting was able to secure the required number of Christian teachers; so the government turned to the Peace Corps.

Another exciting opportunity is the translation and distribution of the Scriptures. Here in this country Bibles and New Testaments are "a dime a dozen," and we have more English versions than we can possibly read. But in many parts of the mission field the churches are still waiting for the Old Testament. Indeed, some of them do not have the complete New Testament.

---

[13] Jennifer Weller, *Africa Now* (September-October 1973), p. 12.

When the New Testament in the Bassa language of Liberia went on sale for the first time in 1971 the people danced in the streets, and the Christian Literature Crusade Bookstore had to lock the iron burglar grill across the doorway and sell the books through the grillwork. Missionary Dave Stull said, "It looked like the New York Stock Exchange. We sold 300 copies in the first fifteen minutes."[14] June Hobley, the missionary who translated the Bassa New Testament, was hugged and greeted by the buyers. Later the CLC bookmobile headed for an inland market and sold its entire supply of six hundred New Testaments in one day.

Never in the history of the Christian church has the demand for the Word of God been as great as it is today. Kenneth Taylor's *Living Bible* first appeared in July 1971. By 1980 it had sold over twenty-five million copies. *Good News for Modern Man*, the New Testament in today's English published by the American Bible Society, first went on sale in the mid-1960s. In the first decade it sold over fifty-five million copies. The *Good News Bible*, released December 1976, sold one million copies the first month.

In 1980 the American Bible Society distributed eighty million copies of the Scriptures. The Bible Society's latest plan is to raise sixty-three million dollars over the next twelve years to help newly literate people around the world improve their reading ability. *Good News for New Readers* will involve the production and distribution of 725 million Bible stories in four-page illustrated leaflet form. These were translated into 348 languages by the end of 1980. It is by far the most ambitious program ever undertaken by the Bible Society in its 165 years of history, challenging every man and resource the Society has.

Scripture distribution in 1980 reached an all-time high of 440 million copies around the world. In Eastern Europe the Scriptures are being printed and sold by the state. In 1980 Scripture distribution increased 82 percent in the Middle East, 117 percent in Mexico, 155 percent in Iran, and 522 percent in Czechoslovakia.

For the first time in history the Roman Catholic Church is actively engaged in Scripture distribution. The Catholic Church still wields enormous influence in parts of the world; with a concentrated promotional effort it can place the Bible in the hands of a multitude of people, especially in Latin America, who do not now possess one. The Archbishop of Asunción authorized the distribution of Scriptures among the pilgrims who gathered at the Sanctuary of Our Lady of Caacupe in 1980. On the same occasion the Bishop of Caacupe over the radio encouraged all Roman Catholics to read the Bible.

A new and fascinating project has been promoted by Rochunga

---

[14] Dave Stull, *Africa Now* (September-October 1971), p. 12.

Pudaite, Director of Bibles for the World, Inc. The idea is to send copies of the New Testament to all persons in the Third World whose names appear in the telephone directories. Already 1,500,000 New Testaments have been mailed to India. The attractive cover, with a picture of the beautiful Taj Mahal and the title *Love Is the Greatest,* makes a strong cultural appeal to the people of India. The response has been remarkable. At one time the office in New Delhi was receiving a thousand letters of appreciation each day. On his last visit to India Mr. Pudaite placed a small ad in a New Delhi newspaper, inviting those who had received copies of his book to come to an auditorium to meet him and to hear the story of his life. Two hours ahead of time the large auditorium was packed. These were all upper-class people, people in a position to afford telephone service. At the close of the address an invitation was given to all who wanted to know more about Jesus Christ and the Bible to come to the front. Half the audience responded. A unique feature of this New Testament is that the Gospel of John comes first because it, more than Matthew, appeals to the Hindu mind.

Another very fruitful form of missionary activity is Bible correspondence courses. One of the earliest courses was *Light of Life,* initiated by Dr. Don Hillis in India back in the 1940s. It began with one course in the Gospel of John in Marathi. Today its five basic courses (John, Acts, Galatians, Mark, and Luke) are available in 70 languages. To date three and a half million persons have received the initial lessons. Of these, 625,000 have completed one or more courses. The Emmaus Bible Correspondence School has produced sixty different courses which have been translated into 120 languages. Some six million persons have enrolled in these courses.

Bible correspondence courses are particularly effective in Muslim countries, where the people are afraid to identify with the Christian church. Over twenty thousand Muslims in Tunisia and an equal number in Morocco have signed up for courses sponsored by the North Africa Mission and the Gospel Missionary Union respectively. So popular were these courses that the government of Tunisia closed the bookstore from which the courses were sent. The operation was moved to France, where it became part of the Radio School of the Bible's outreach. In Iran the requests for Bible correspondence courses were so numerous that missionaries had to be taken off other jobs to cope with the mail. Since the liberation of Bangladesh over twelve thousand persons, most of them Muslims, have signed up for Bible courses. In six months time the missionary staff was increased from one to six. Even so it has not been possible to keep up with the demand.

Missionary radio is another exciting field in which to labor. There are today some sixty radio stations owned and operated by Christian missions in all parts of the world. Half a dozen of them are very large

102 / THE MAKING OF A MISSIONARY

and powerful. These include Station ELWA in Liberia; Station HCJB in Ecuador; Far East Broadcasting Company in Manila, Korea, Saipan, and Seychelles Islands; Trans World Radio in Monaco, Bonaire, Sri Lanka, Cyprus, Guam, and Swaziland; and TEAM in Korea. Some of these stations have more than three hundred members on the staff, including nationals as well as missionaries. Two of them operate a hospital in connection with their work. Several of them have a Bible Institute of the Air by means of which they do follow-up work. In addition there are hundreds of missionaries and nationals producing radio and television programs for broadcasting over commercial and government stations. This is a wide-open field and one that requires highly trained technical personnel not always easy to recruit.

A new and rapidly developing field is Christian journalism. Most missions are weak in this area and the national churches are almost completely destitute of well-trained journalists. With tens of millions of new literates in the world every year, and with the governments of the Third World in some cases devoting 20 to 30 percent of the national budget to education, it goes without saying that both church and mission must produce more and better literature than in the past. The most desperate need is for professional missionary-journalists who can train nationals to produce good, attractive, well-written literature in the vernacular.

These are days of great opportunity. The doors that are open are *wide* open. People the world over are receptive as they have never been before. The fields are indeed white unto harvest. Bill Bright, President of Campus Crusade for Christ, returning from a world tour, had this to say: "The more I see of what God is doing in the world, the more I am convinced that we stand today, *at this very hour,* on the threshold of the greatest spiritual advance the world has ever witnessed. Clearly God is telling us that tens of millions are ready and waiting to know Jesus Christ."[15]

Campus Crusade for Christ, the fastest growing Christian organization in the world, has sixty-three hundred staff members, half of which are nationals overseas. Its latest venture is the Agape Movement, a ministry that is designed to recruit and train 100,000 men and women to give two years or more of their lives to sharing God's love with the people in more than two million villages, cities, and university centers all over the world by 1980.

Another aggressive group is Wycliffe Bible Translators, whose missionaries are now at work in 750 tribes in forty-one countries of the world. There are still more than 3,300 tribes without any portion of the Word of God. WBT intends to zero in on those 200 million

---

[15] Bill Bright, *Christmas Letter,* 1973.

people. To this end they are expanding their work with every passing month. Their ultimate goal is to complete the task by the end of the century.

The Unfinished Task

Before we can decide whether a task is finished or unfinished it is necessary to define both its nature and extent. What is the extent of the Christian mission? It is coterminous with the world. It is a global task. We have been commanded by the Lord Jesus Christ to go into *all* the world, to preach the gospel to *every* creature, and to make disciples of *all* nations. And when we get through we shall have in the church converts "from every tribe and tongue and people and nation" (Re 5:9). This gospel must be preached in all the world. Then, and only then, will the end come (Mt 24:14). This is the extent of the task.

What is the nature of the task? Is it to civilize, to Christianize, or to evangelize the world? Obviously it is not to civilize, for large portions of the world were civilized long before we were. Nor is it to Christianize, for even that part of the world that we identify as Christendom has not been completely Christianized. There is nothing in Scripture or history to support the view that the entire world is going to be converted to Jesus Christ—at least not in this age. We are left, then, with world evangelization. That, without doubt, is the supreme. task of the church.

But this poses another question. What are we to understand by the term "evangelization?" Or to put it more concretely: When is a country or a people evangelized? When they have heard the gospel once? Twice? Ten times? A hundred times? When the Bible has been translated? When a church has been established?

A people may be said to be evangelized when everyone has had the gospel presented to him often enough and clearly enough to enable him to make an intelligent response for or against Jesus Christ as Savior and Lord.

There are, of course, degrees of evangelization. Not everyone in a given society will be equally knowledgeable, even though all have the same access to knowledge. There are still some people in the United States who do not know who Henry Kissinger is and others who have never heard of Johnny Carson. The same applies to a knowledge of the gospel. Even here in the United States there are millions of persons who have never seen a copy of the Bible or attended a church service. Indeed, some have never heard the name of Christ except as a curse word. If this is true, then even the United States is still unevangelized even though the Bible is the best seller year after year and the Christian church is the largest and most influential institution in the country.

There is another aspect of the problem of world evangelization. It is not something that can be achieved once and for all. Every generation needs to be evangelized all over again, for every thirty years we have an entirely new group of people. One generation may be predominantly Christian while the following one is only nominally so. This in turn may be followed by a third generation that is more pagan than Christian. In the history of the church there have been times of renewal and advance and there have been periods of stagnation and decline. Nothing can be taken for granted. The candlestick may be removed and the church left without light. Or the church may be disobedient and allowed to go into captivity. The church that fails to live by the law of God will find itself under the judgment of God.

This may be happening right under our eyes. We are now talking about a "post-Christian era" here in the West. It may be that God's center of gravity is about to shift from the West to the East. By the end of this century it is quite possible that Africa may be a predominantly Christian continent and Europe virtually pagan. And the United States may not be far behind.

> In thinking about the Church it is easy to slip into the erroneous idea that, because a country or parish has once been Christian it will remain so until the end of time. . . . One generation succeeds to another, and that which comes is not naturally and inevitably Christian. . . . The task of the Church must always be unfinished, because so much energy must go into the endless business of winning the younger generation for Christ.[16]

So we see that the task of world evangelization has two aspects. It is perennial and universal at the same time. For this reason the task is never finished.

If the task remains unfinished, it is only right to ask: What remains to be done? The answer is: Plenty.

The population of the world now stands at 4.5 billion and is increasing at the amazing rate of 80 million every year. In round figures *approximately* 26 percent of the world's population are professing Christians—more than half of them Roman Catholics. Another third has been exposed to the Christian message in one form or another but has failed to respond affirmatively. Another third has yet to hear the name of Jesus Christ for the first time.

Every concerned Christian must agree that there is little comfort to be derived from those statistics. In spite of the enormous amount of time, energy, and money that have gone into the Christian mission in the last 275 years we are not quite holding our own. In 1960 Christians

[16] Stephen Neill, *The Unfinished Task* (London: Edinburgh House Press, 1957), p. 35.

represented about 34 percent of the world's population. Today the ratio is closer to 26 percent, *and dropping slowly every year*. Black Africa is the only continent where we are making significant gains; but these are more than offset by the losses suffered in the vast continent of Asia, where more than half the world's population is located.

In the Muslim world, where there are over 700 million souls, we have yet to achieve anything resembling a breakthrough, except in Indonesia, where on the island of Java several hundred thousand Muslims have come to Christ. In all other Muslim countries converts are hand-picked, one by one, and a public baptism is a rare phenomenon. Bangladesh, the second largest Muslim country in the world, is now a secular state. It remains to be seen to what extent this will facilitate missionary work.

In Asia there is only one predominantly Christian country—the Philippines, where 81 percent of the people are Roman Catholics and 8 or 10 percent are Protestants. We are making significant progress in several other countries. We are doing exceedingly well in Korea, where approximately 20 to 22 percent of the population are professing Christians. A people movement in Taiwan has brought most of the 250,000 animistic tribespeople into the Christian fold; but the Taiwanese, like Buddhists elsewhere, have not responded in anything like the same manner.

In the other countries of Asia we are barely holding our own; in some we are actually falling behind. In India, with 680 million souls, the Christians represent about 2.9 percent of the population. That ratio has not changed significantly in the last twenty years. The situation in Communist China is difficult to evaluate precisely. In 1950, the last year for which we have reliable statistics, the total number of Christians was four million, of whom three million were Roman Catholics. During the last thirty years the Christians in China have been cut off from all contact with the churches in the West. For a time we feared that Christianity had received a mortal blow, but recent reports indicate that the church is alive and well, though most of the believers are without Bibles.

Another large country is Japan with 116 million people, of whom only 1 million are professing Christians. In Burma the tribal churches, without missionaries since 1966, are thriving; but the Burmese Buddhists, who form well over 95 percent of the population, are practically untouched. In Thailand, the only other large country in that part of the world, there is 1 Christian to every 999 Buddhists. Like Goliath of old the great ethnic religions of Asia are still defying the armies of the living God. We still have a long way to go before Asia's more than 2 billion people are evangelized.

In Africa the picture is much brighter. Here is the one major region of the world where Christianity is forging ahead with such vigor that

some experts are predicting that by the year 2000 Africa will be a predominantly Christian continent. Already Christians represent 50 percent of the total population of Black Africa—everything south of the
Sahara Desert. We have often been told that the Muslims are making
converts faster than we are. That may have been true ten or twenty
years ago; it is true no longer. Christians in Black Africa now outnumber the Muslims by 75 million. In some countries the Christians
now represent anywhere from 75 to 95 percent of the population.
In the largest country, Nigeria, the Christian ratio has climbed rapidly
in the last decade to 46 percent, two percentage points ahead of
the Muslims. Animism, now referred to as "traditional religion," is
on the way out; and the battle for the soul of Africa is between Christianity and Islam, with Christianity having the edge.

In Latin America the situation is unique. The Protestants, especially
the Pentecostals, are registering fantastic gains in such countries as
Brazil, Chile, and Colombia. In 1900 there were fifty thousand Protestants in Latin America. By 1950 the number had climbed to ten million.
Twenty years later the figure had doubled to twenty million. Today
it is closer to twenty-five million.

It must be remembered, however, that almost all of these converts have come from a nominally Catholic background; so the overall
picture of Christianity versus "heathenism" is not appreciably altered
by the tremendous growth of evangelical Christianity in Latin America.
The Roman Catholic Church dominates the religious scene in that part
of the world and claims 90 percent of the people as adherents; but
by its own confession very few of them—perhaps 10 percent—are
practicing Catholics. This has left them wide open to the overtures of
the gospel as presented by the Evangelicals.

Europe and North America are also part of the mission field. They
too should be included in the tally. An estimated 160 million people
in Europe make no profession of religion. The two big denominations
are the Lutherans on the continent and the Anglicans in the United
Kingdom. In both Communions membership is down and the bottom
has dropped out of church attendance. By no stretch of the imagination
can Europe be called a Christian continent. This is one area of the
world where Christianity seems to be losing ground.

In North America the scene is considerably brighter; but even here
there is cause for concern. The main-line denominations, which represent the majority of Protestants, are reducing their staffs and slashing
their budgets, particularly that portion that relates to foreign missions.
The conservative denominations and the many independent churches
are growing; but because they are small their growth hardly makes up
for the decline in the main-line churches. Church membership in the
United States remains fairly steady year after year, about 63 percent;

and church attendance is high as compared with Europe—60 percent for the Catholics, 40 percent for the Protestants, and 25 percent for the Jews.

We are grateful to God for the growth of the Christian Church in many parts of the world; at the same time we are painfully aware of certain elements and areas of weakness. Many of the older churches stand in need of revival if they are ever to assume their role in the evangelization of the world. It is commonly known that the most zealous Christians are first-generation believers, whose conversion experience is generally very meaningful. There is often a noticeable cooling off in second- and third-generation Christians.

After describing the remarkable ministry of Bishop Azariah of Dornakal, Stephen Neill goes on to say: "The work in Dornakal was very far from perfect. As we have already seen, at the end of his life Bishop Azariah was distressed to find in the second and third generations of Christians so much less zeal and devotion than he had hoped for."[17]

After the second or third generation Christianity tends to take on cultural overtones, and its adherents lose all desire to share their faith with friends and neighbors. The churches then become so moribund that their chief preoccupation is not the salvation of the lost but their own survival.

In the older regions of the mission field there are thousands of such churches that need to be revived. If these churches with their well-educated pastors and their highly literate, and sometimes wealthy, congregations could be revived they could easily spearhead an evangelistic thrust that would be felt throughout the whole of the Third World. During the 1940s John Sung was mightily used of God to revive the older Chinese churches in Southeast Asia. In every church he formed an evangelistic band, which helped to keep the revival fires burning. To this day the older members of those churches still talk of John Sung and his powerful ministry. One revivalist like John Sung or Jonathan Goforth can do more for the evangelization of the world than ten evangelists who win converts but fail to revive the churches.[18]

The churches in the Third World are not the only ones that need to be revived. The sending churches in the West have the same problem. They too have a tendency to cool off in the second and third generations. Indeed, every movement secular or sacred tends to revert to type with the passing of time. Even the Communists are not immune to this kind of problem. The Cultural Revolution in China in 1966 was

[17] Stephen Neill, *The Unfinished Task* (London: Edinburgh House Press, 1957), p. 129.
[18] For the ministry of these two men see Leslie Lyall, *John Sung: Flame for God in the Far East* (Chicago: Moody Press, 1956); and Jonathan Goforth, *By My Spirit* (Grand Rapids: Zondervan, 1942).

an attempt on the part of Mao Tse-tung to stem the rising tide of bourgeois thinking that was beginning to reappear in Chinese society, after only seventeen years.

There is a good deal of dead wood in our American churches. It is not uncommon for a church with 2,500 members to have only 750 present on Sunday morning. In our larger denominations the average church member gives only eight dollars a year to world missions. On the other hand some of the younger and smaller denominations are giving four and five times that much. Throughout history revival and missions have always gone together. When the former ceases, the latter is sure to languish. At home or overseas the churches stand in need of continuing renewal.

Closely allied to the revival of the churches is a crying need for a spiritual ministry to the pastors throughout the Third World. There are tens of thousands of these faithful men serving small, struggling, semiliterate congregations. Most of them are underpaid and overworked. They are constantly giving out; seldom do they have an opportunity to take in. Their entire "library" may occupy less than two feet of shelf space. They shepherd small flocks in the midst of a predominantly non-Christian culture. They have no one with whom they can share their burdens. Often they become weary and discouraged.

World Vision International has done more than any other group to minister to the spiritual needs of these pastors. In twenty-two years it has conducted eighty-one pastors' conferences with a total attendance of 56,268. Pastors from all denominations are invited to a central place for a week or ten days of rich ministry by such outstanding Bible teachers as Paul Rees, Chandu Ray, Carl Henry, and others. All travel expenses are paid; room and board are provided free. All the pastors have to do is to attend the meetings, enjoy the fellowship, and drink in the exposition of the Word. For many of these men a gathering of this kind is like a blood transfusion. They return to their churches refreshed and invigorated in body, mind, and spirit. Only eternity will reveal what has been accomplished by these conferences. This is a vital ministry that should by all means be continued in the future.

Another unfinished task is theological education. We rejoice when Dr. George Peters tells us that the non-Christian peoples of the world are more eager to hear the gospel than we are to preach it; but the mushroom growth in evidence in some countries is a cause for deep concern. In Latin America some sixty thousand leaders who function as pastors in the churches have had little or no Bible training. Only fifteen thousand out of the seventy-five thousand church leaders have had what might be termed adequate theological training. Only in half a dozen countries—Japan and Korea among them—is there anything like a sufficient number of trained pastors. In other countries it is not uncommon for one man to have the oversight of ten or more congregations.

Only in recent years has a concerted effort been made to meet this appalling need. The new program known as Theological Education by Extension had its origin in Latin America in 1960. It is still too early to know how effective it will be; but preliminary reports are most encouraging. This is an ongoing task. It will take us many years to provide the Third World churches with a sufficient number of fully trained pastors.

Another part of the unfinished task is pioneer work. With today's emphasis on the rapidly developing national churches and the talk about urbanization and its effect on Christian missions, there is a prevailing notion that there is no more pioneer work to be done. Nothing could be further from the truth. Indeed, one outstanding missiologist reminds us that "the greater part of the missionary work that ought to be carried on is still pioneer work."[19] The most recent thrust in missions is a worldwide call to pioneer evangelism. Ralph Winter and his colleagues at the United States Center for World Mission in Pasadena, California, have located 16,750 unreached groups all over the world. Known as "Hidden People," they are said to be beyond the reach of any existing church or mission. Already the idea is catching on and many missions and churches are rearranging their priorities and gearing up for pioneer evangelism. The watchword of the movement is, "A church for every people by the year 2000." It remains to be seen whether the Christian Church of the twentieth century has the determination and the dynamism to achieve this ambitious goal, truly a monumental challenge.

David Barrett reminds us that of 860 tribes in Africa, 213 are completely or heavily Muslim and have virtually no Christian witness. In addition there are still 236 tribes largely unevangelized, representing 13 percent of the population. There are still tribes in the great Amazon Basin that have yet to establish contact with the outside world.

There are infant churches in the pioneer areas without leadership that are calling for outside help. Such a plea came recently from Nagaland in northeast India:

> We send you greetings in the name of Jesus Christ. We are all fine. We have accepted the Faith since 1969. No one ever taught us about Christ. But we were hungry for the eternal message. Fourteen villages have accepted the Faith. The present membership is 1,112. There are still countless people who want to become Christian, but there is no one who knows the Bible well. . . . We have been looking for a missionary family who could live

---

[19] Stephen Neill, *Call to Mission* (Philadelphia: Fortress Press, 1970), p. 101.

with us and teach us daily. We are also looking for someone who could help us in medical treatment. We have been waiting such a long period for someone, but still not a single person has come to teach us.[20]

There are still areas of the world where the Christian presence is either very weak or nonexistent: Sikkim, Bhutan, Saudi Arabia, Mauritania, Afghanistan, Nepal, and Somalia. The Christian church should not rest content until all these countries are open to the gospel. And what shall be said about China with its 980 million souls living under a Communist government that is bent on the ultimate destruction of all forms of religion? Now that China seems to be turning its face once again toward the West, the Christian church throughout the world should make the evangelization of that immense country a matter of long and earnest prayer.

Still largely neglected are the intellectuals in the Third World. In the past missionaries, for reasons not altogether invalid, ministered almost exclusively to the lower classes. This is one reason, though not the only one, why so many national churches today lack well-educated leaders. Now that higher education is available to the masses, it is imperative that we give more attention to the evangelization of the intellectual classes, especially the students on the university campuses. In some of the large cities of the Third World, Tokyo, Manila, Jakarta, and Calcutta, there are dozens of colleges and universities and tens of thousands of students. The Christian witness in these institutions comes almost entirely from the outside, sponsored largely by such groups as Campus Crusade, Inter-Varsity Christian Fellowship, International Fellowship of Evangelical Students, Navigators, and others. An IFES staff worker reports that there are 700,000 students in forty-four universities in Italy; but committed Christians number fewer than fifty. The ratio wouldn't be any better in France.

There are two ways to have an effective witness in these secular universities of the Third World. Nonprofessional missionaries with advanced degrees could seek teaching positions in these institutions. Once on the faculty these dedicated Christians could have a most effective ministry, to some extent in the classroom (depending on the subjects taught) and certainly in social intercourse outside the classroom. A second method would be for the missions to establish hostels, with or without boarding facilities, in close proximity to the universities. Christian students needing fellowship and moral support could live at the hostel and study in the university. Others could visit the hostel, play games, read periodicals, listen to good music, engage in rap sessions, Bible study, etc. From the long-range point of view it is more

[20]Church Growth Bulletin, Vol. X, No. 1 (September 1973), p. 360.

advantageous to win one university student than to win half a dozen peasants who can neither read nor write.

No church can ever become permanently strong and virile without the Scriptures in its own tongue. This was one reason for the demise of the large church in North Africa at the time of the Muslim invasion. One of the greatest achievements of the missionaries has been the translation of the Scriptures into over seventeen hundred languages. This represents a monumental piece of work, and the churches of the Third World are forever indebted to them and the Bible societies for giving them the Bible in their own tongue at a price they can afford to pay.

A closer look at the situation will reveal the fact that of these 1,710 translations, only 275 involve the entire Bible and another 495 the New Testament. The remaining 940 translations are single Books, called Portions. This means that in spite of all that has been done there are many large churches on the mission field that are still without the New Testament. It is difficult for us in the West to visualize a Church of ten thousand members without a complete Bible. But such a phenomenon is by no means uncommon on the mission field.

Wycliffe Bible Translators has done yeoman service in this area. Since the beginning in 1935 translators have worked in 902 tribes and produced Scriptures in most of those languages. To date Wycliffe has produced complete New Testaments in 150 languages—twenty-four in 1980 alone. Its translators make it a practice to remain in one tribe only until the New Testament is translated, then they move on to another tribe and repeat the performance there. In this way they hope to cover every tribe by the year 2000. They still have some 3,300 tribes to contact. It is estimated that these tribes represent about 200 million people. Even if they achieve their goal, they will have given these tribes only the New Testament. They will still need The Old Testament.

Whenever Bible translation is mentioned we naturally think of first-time translations. These, of course, are very important, but they are not the whole story. Languages change as we have good cause to know. When they change significantly a new translation of the Scriptures is needed. This is called revision rather than translation. At the present time the United Bible Societies are working with some three thousand missionary-linguists at work on some eight hundred different projects, most of them revisions of earlier translations. This is a never-ending task.

The production of Christian literature is another facet of the unfinished task. In addition to the Scriptures the churches and their leaders need a long list of helps: hymnbooks; commentaries; dictionaries; study, devotional, and expository books; Sunday school and Christian education materials; periodicals; audio-visual aids, and a hundred-and-one other helps that can be found in any Christian bookstore in the United States.

Here in this country every major denomination has its own hymnal, its own Sunday school materials, and in many cases its own publishing house. If a Sunday school superintendent runs out of materials he has only to drop a postcard in the mail on Monday and the desired materials will be on hand for the following Sunday. Would to God it were that simple on the mission field! The average American church member cannot possibly visualize what Christian work is like in many parts of the mission field. The difference between the services and facilities available there and those available here is like the difference between the old general store and the modern supermarket. There is no comparison.

Imagine trying to teach Sunday school without any helps at all, or trying to prepare a sermon without a single commentary or expository book. It's done all the time on the mission field, not by choice but of necessity. Many a pastor has only the notes he acquired in Bible school—if indeed he ever went to Bible school. In preparing for his Sunday morning service he must rely on his own knowledge of the Scriptures. Little wonder that some of them fall back on dreams and visions.

Is the task of world evangelization completed? From all four corners of the earth comes a resounding *No!* Far from being completed, we have hardly reached the halfway point. To quit now would jeopardize the entire enterprise.

Select Bibliography

Adeney, David H. *China: Christian Students Face the Revolution.* Downers Grove, IL : Inter-Varsity Press, 1973.

Broomhall, A. J. *Time for Action.* London: Inter-Varsity Fellowship, 1965.

Cable, Mildred and French, Francesca. *Ambassadors for Christ.* Chicago: Moody Press, 1935.

Cannon, Joseph L. *For Missionaries Only.* Grand Rapids: Baker Book House, 1969.

Coggins, Wade T. *So That's What Missions Is All About.* Chicago: Moody Press, 1975.

Collins, Marjorie A. *Manual for Accepted Candidates.* South Pasadena, CA : William Carey Library, 1973.

————. *Who Cares About the Missionary?* Chicago: Moody Press, 1974.

Clark, Dennis E. *The Third World and Mission.* Waco, TX: Word Books, 1971.

Cook, Harold R. *Missionary Life and Work.* Chicago: Moody Press, 1959.

Exley, Helen and Richard. *In Search of the Missionary.* London: Highway Press, 1970.

Fenton, Horace L., Jr. *Myths About Missions.* Downers Grove, IL : Inter-Varsity Press, 1973.

Griffiths, Michael. *Who Really Sends the Missionary?* Chicago: Moody Press, 1972.

Hillis, Don W. *I Don't Feel Called (Thank the Lord!).* Wheaton, IL : Tyndale House, 1973.

Houghton, A. T. *Preparing to Be a Missionary.* London: Inter-Varsity Press, 1956.

Howard, David M. *Student Power in World Evangelism.* Downers Grove, IL : Inter-Varsity Press, 1970.

Griffiths, Michael. *Give Up Your Small Ambitions.* London: Inter-Varsity Press, 1970.

Kane, J. Herbert. *Winds of Change in the Christian Mission.* Chicago: Moody Press, 1973.

————. *Understanding Christian Missions.* Grand Rapids: Baker Book House, 1974.

McGavran, Donald, (ed.). *Crucial Issues in Missions Tomorrow.* Chicago: Moody Press, 1972.

Morgan, G. Helen. *Who'd Be a Missionary?* Fort Washington, PA: Christian Literature Crusade, 1972.

Neill, Stephen. *Call to Mission.* Philadelphia: Fortress Press, 1971.

Peters, George W. *A Biblical Theology of Missions.* Chicago: Moody Press, 1972.

Sargent, Douglas N. *The Making of a Missionary.* London: Hodder and Stoughton, 1960.

Soltau, T. Stanley. *Facing the Field.* Grand Rapids: Baker Book House, 1959.

Trueblood, Elton. *The Validity of the Christian Mission.* New York: Harper and Row, 1972.

Tuggy, Joy T. *The Missionary Wife and Her Work.* Chicago: Moody Press, 1966.

Wagner, C. Peter. *Stop the World I Want to Get On.* Glendale, CA : Regal Books, 1973.

Williamson, Mabel. *Have We No Right?* Chicago: Moody Press, 1957.

Winter, Ralph D. *The Twenty-Five Unbelievable Years, 1945-1969.* South Pasadena, CA.: William Carey Library, 1970.

Wong, James, et al. *Missions from the Third World.* Singapore: Church Growth Study Center, 1973.